THERE ARE CHARISMS AND CHARISMS

The Religious Life

J.M.R. TILLARD, O.P.

There are Charisms and Charisms

THE RELIGIOUS LIFE

Translated from the French by Olga Prendergast, M.A.

LUMEN VITAE

184, rue Washington, 1050 Bruxelles

CONTENTS

Foreword 11

Chapter I 29

Beyond Purely Moral Motivations 29

A Charismatic Call and Project 35

A God-Centred Wonder : a Decision « because
of Christ » 46

The Vow as the Gift of Self : Confession and
Adoration 60

Contemplative Attention and the « Following of
Christ 65

Chapter II 71

The Search for God 71

The Monastic Aim 76

« Following of Christ, » Search for God, Monastic Aim 100

Chapter III 109

The Confession of Faith as a State of Being :
Witnessing among Men, before God . . 110

The Confession of Faith at the Service of Humanity, before God 117

From the State of Confession of Faith to the
Word of Confession 127

Conclusion 137

To my friends of the « Charismatic Renewal » who allowed me to challenge them in a brotherly spirit, and thus furthered my understanding :

Maurice, Alain, Michel, Maurice, Daniel, Michel of the *Dominican College of Theology of Ottawa* ;

Nicholas, Michael, Alan, David, John, Ken and Dennis of the *St John's College of Theology in Nottingham.*

Over the past few years the Christian Churches have been taking a fresh interest in the experience of God. After the endless debates on secularization, the « Death of God » theologies and a somewhat suspicious approach to contemplation, prayers groups are being formed practically everywhere and « renewal » movements are flourishing, bringing together Catholic and Protestant laymen, priests and religious. Christians, eagerly joining in a search launched mainly by monastic communities, are beginning to practise yoga, Zen and transcendental meditation with the aim of « relearning the ways of contemplation. » And while the religious congregations dedicated to action see their novitiates steadily shrinking for lack of new members, foundations centred on silence and prayer are attracting young Christians in both the Reformed Churches and the Catholic Church. In Greece, too, there is a renewed interest in the monastic life. [1] One of the most salient features of modern theological thinking, however, is the emphasis laid on the person of the Holy Spirit. He

---

1. See « L'Eglise en Grèce, » in *Pro Mundi Vita : Dossiers*, Nov. 1976, 13-20.

is no longer the great « forgotten one. » A sensible person
might even feel that today he is too often highlighted :
Christians are invoking him on every conceivable occa-
sion, sometimes attributing to his immediate influence certain phenomena or attitudes that a more critical judgment
would hesitate to ascribe to anything more mysterious than
an explosion of religious sentiment.

One epithet usually qualifies this lively spiritual enthusiasm. Everywhere Christians are speaking of the « charismatic » renewal, movement and manifestation. Inevitably the term is engendering a certain confusion.
Obviously we recognize in the adjective « charismatic »
the word *charis* signifying grace, and especially the Greek
noun *charisma* which, as St Paul tells us, denotes the
gratuitous gifts of the Spirit (plural : *charismata,* or more
commonly « charisms »). In itself the label « charismatic »
therefore encompasses a wide range of spiritual experiences : surges of religious fervour, a collective or individual return to the evangelical attitude. Unquestionably,
these are signs of grace, as none may doubt in God's
Church. The adjective « charismatic » is indeed so intimately associated with grace that it is heartening to see
it once again becoming foremost in the Christian consciousness. The problem is that certain groups have, so
to speak, appropriated it, thus restricting its meaning.
And whereas its use should remind us of the situation
of every baptized person who is faithful to his baptismal
grace, the word has assumed sectarian undertones in the
minds of many Christians. As they see it, there are the
« charismatics » and... the « others, » who are, of course,
baptized in water and in the Spirit, but not really *seized*
by the Spirit.

Indeed, in popular accounts it has nowadays become quite usual to reserve the adjective « *charismatic* » for a particular type of Christian experience. This experience is linked with an extraordinary manifestation of gifts, attributed to the outpouring of the Spirit : glossolalia, interpretation, prophecy, healing. It is often seen as the unequivocal expression of the presence of God's Spirit, a highly desirable expression, an almost certain sign of entry into the mystery of the new Covenant. In classical pentecostalism, but also in the view of some Catholic and Protestant groups, this outpouring of the Spirit and of his gifts is, moreover, intrinsically linked with what is called « baptism in the Spirit, » which — as some confidently affirm — is either the real awakening or the completion of our common baptism in water. Christian baptism, they say, is too ritualized and, being usually received before the age of reason, it is too remote from a real conversion to the Gospel : therefore it cannot have the « full » effect of grace. Hence the pentecostal laying-on of hands would enable the Spirit to exercise the fullness of his power in those mediocre and hitherto slumbering Christian lives. From there it is but one step to assuming that the field of the authentic charismatic experience more or less coincides with that of the pentecostal experience...

Now that is an extraordinarily myopic view. And equally astonishing is the widely held opinion that if the Church is now restoring the Spirit to his rightful place in her life of faith, this is mainly due to the « charismatic renewal », understood in the narrow sense. Those who hold this opinion are overlooking the influence of the patristic renewal and ecumenical dialogue with the

Eastern Church. They have failed to note how significant, at this level, is the introduction of the epiclesis —
the explicit and unequivocal invocation — in the new
eucharistic canons of the Catholic Church, therefore in
the very heart of the central action of her life. Indeed,
the epiclesis had been readopted long before the charismatic movement was as prominent as it now is. For the
epiclesis is the invocation to the Spirit, the prayer whereby we ask him to change the bread and wine into the
Body and Blood of the Lord, so that the lives of those
who communicate in them may be transformed. [2] Thanks
to a closer study of the Greek Fathers, theology now
teaches that the Lord's eucharistic Body is that of the
Risen Christ, the pneumatic Body, transformed by the
Spirit in the paschal event. [3] Moreover, since the turn
of the century the stressing of the central place of the
paschal Mystery has considerably helped to revive the
Christian understanding of the Spirit's unique role : it
is the Spirit who raises the Crucified Jesus to life, and
the wonders of the day of Pentecost are the obverse,
the other side, of the Wonder of Easter morning (Acts
2, 33). Theology's present interest in the Holy Spirit was
already in germ many years ago. It is of some significance
that as early as 1868, G. Moberley gave his famous Oxford

---

2. On this question of the epiclesis and its significance, see L.
BOUYER, *Eucharistie*, Desclée, 1966, especially pp. 300-304 ; also
J.M.R. TILLARD, « L'Eucharistie et le Saint-Esprit, » in NRT 90,
1968, 363-387, and J.H. McKENNA, « The Eucharistic Epiclesis in
Twentieth Century Theology (1900-1966), » in *Ephemerides Litur-
gicae* 90, 1976, 289-328.
3. This is the central theme of my book *L'Eucharistie Pâque de
l'Eglise, Unam Sanctam* series 44, Paris, 1964 (especially 175-212).

lectures on the Spirit and the Body of Christ,[4] that soon after H. B. Swete wrote his ever-topical studies of the Holy Spirit in the New Testament and in the earliest tradition of the Church,[5] and that H. Wheeler Robinson's book on the Christian experience of the Spirit first came out in 1928.[6] The Catholic reader may reply that these were isolated and rarefied theological reflections — and Anglican to boot ! This would be to overlook, for example, that the theme of the 1956 Students' Pilgrimage to Chartres was the Holy Spirit.[7] Enthusiasm for the charismatic renewal should not allow us to disregard the facts or to designate as the cause what is merely an effect.

The above remarks already make clear that if we give the terms their normal meaning, the charismatic life and the experience of the Spirit are infinitely broader than current usage suggests. Every authentic Christian life is a life in the Spirit and fully charismatic, even without glossolalia, prophecy, interpretation or any other extraordinary gift. Every Christian eucharistic assembly is charismatic, even when there is no external manifestation

---

4. G. MOBERLY, *The Administration of the Holy Spirit in the Body of Christ, Bampton Lectures 1868*, London, 1904.
5. H.B. SWETE, *The Holy Spirit in the New Testament*, London, 1909 ; ID., *The Holy Spirit in the Ancient Church*, London, 1912 ; ID., *On the History of the Doctrine of the Procession of the Holy Spirit*, London, 1913.
6. H. WHEELER ROBINSON, *The Christian Experience of the Holy Spirit*, London, 1928.
7. See R. CONGAR's little book, *La Pentecôte. Chartres 1956*, Paris, 1956. More than ten years previously Fr. CONGAR had included in the *Unam Sanctam* series (Nos. 16 and 17) a translation of Dom VONIER, *L'Esprit et l'Epouse*, and a study by P. NAUTIN, *Je crois à l'Esprit Saint dans la Sainte Eglise, pour la résurrection de la chair*.

of the outpouring of the Spirit. Every Christian prayer is a prayer in the Spirit, even without the enthusiasm of a communicative experience. And I venture to add that every Christian suffering lived in Christ is charismatic, even if it is not the object of healing. At another level — that of the distribution of tasks and vocations for the good of the Church — every vocation called to impart growth and splendour to the Body of Christ is charismatic, even if in its daily exercise it has nothing to do with « miraculous » phenomena. In this sense the religious vocation is charismatic *per se,* because of its essential relation to the Lord's Spirit.

It is, of course, undeniable that when the charismatic renewal (in the popular sense) is not too intent on seeking extraordinary or « miraculous » phenomena, it is the sign of a profound need of the People of God. That People is once again thirsting for the transcendent. And its thirst comes from the Spirit. It would be foolish to doubt the genuineness of the need for prayer and the desire to speak of God and of Christ which are re-emerging practically everywhere, and often among people to whom the word « charismatic, » in the current sense, is hardly applicable. Similarly, it would be unpardonable to state bluntly, without further qualification, that the pentecostalism of Catholic, Protestant or Anglican groups underestimates sacramental baptism. For the great majority of its followers, the charismatic movement simply expresses a sincere desire to renew the inner life, and more particularly the experience of God. This is surely a matter for rejoicing. Objectively speaking, it is a way of actualizing the life in the Spirit which is communicated by baptism and ceaselessly nourished by communion in the Lord's

eucharistic body. One cannot but rejoice to see Christians
thus discovering a path of grace. Besides, every epoch has
known kindred spiritual movements that revitalize fervent
Christian groups. We have only to think of the influence
of the eucharistic devotion in the last century and at the
beginning of this century.

*

*   *

The problem begins when, like certain movements
which preceded it, the charismatic renewal presents itself
as an absolute. And especially when it refuses to be
challenged or criticized. Now even those who sympathize
with it are beginning to be worried about the lack of
theological humour and critical spirit that seems to prevail
in certain tendencies of the renewal.[8] Let us not be disturbed by the fact that Christians, caught up in the enthusiasm of collective prayer, are speaking in tongues, and
let us try to adopt St Paul's tolerant attitude. Life in the
Spirit espouses the laws of human psychology, including
man's passions and emotions. But the theologian feels
somewhat uneasy when that same glossolalia is presented
to him as « the supreme form of prayer in the Spirit, with
its ineffable undertones », and certain believers refuse to
admit that such a phenomenon (even in an assembly)
may not always be the fruit of the Spirit. In Paul's day
glossolalia was already known outside Christianity... By

8. See, for example, J.R. BOUCHET and H. CAFFAREL, *Le
renouveau charismatique interpellé, études et documents*, Paris, 1976.
A book discussed further on in the present study.

the same token, a Christian admits the possibility of the
miracle and recognizes with the Christian Tradition that the
sacrament of anointing the sick can have a healing effect
on the mind or the body. But if he has any critical judgment at all, he nonetheless pleads for common sense when
he hears about certain healing sessions. In this domain
the forces of the psyche may be misleading, and it is well
known that the miracles at Lourdes, for example, are
recognized and declared with great prudence. The same
holds true of prophecy and interpretation. Who can be
certain that — even in an experience of charismatic
fervour — the interpretation given, which can sometimes
unsettle a whole life, comes from the Spirit ? We know
only too well how often certain illuminates, unaware of
their own condition, find a privileged audience in a fervent
religious circle. It is not without relevance that pastoral
theology has always stressed the necessity of spiritual
discernment, which is not to be confused with the gym-
nastics of casuistry. The phenomena appreciated by the
charismatic renewal belong to a domain that easily involves
illusion. When people are advised to be less credulous and
less anxious to look for marvels, they generally agree in
principle ? But what happens in practice ?

Then there is an even more complex problem to be faced.
For some Christians intensely involved in the charismatic
movement — be they laymen, religious or ministers — the
type of experience which this movement affords becomes
not an aid to living more authentically the communion
with God inherent in their own vocation, but the supreme
experience to which everything else must be subordinated.
Nowadays I am encountering more and more young religious, monks and nuns, even contemplatives, who affirm

that since they have experienced charismatic prayer, every other form of prayer seems empty to them. They feel that even the divine office has become insipid, with the result that the liturgy of the community or the monastery is gradually becoming a kind of formal exercise in which they participate only because they are obliged to do so. Admittedly, the post-conciliar liturgical renewal has been too centred on a return to pure forms that are highly traditional but do not sufficiently embrace life and concrete experience. But the fact remains that the great liturgical prayer of the Church is of inestimable value : it transcends the participants' particular needs and feelings but expresses the objective thanksgiving and intercession of God's People by readopting psalms that go back to far-distant times and are mellowed by centuries and centuries of praise and anguish. How then, especially if one is a contemplative or a cleric, can one not strive to understand that great prayer and to accord it its rightful place, a central place, even if, personally, one does not always manage to be on the same wave-length ? The prayer of the universal Church infinitely surpasses each individual who offers it up : it calls him to poverty of heart. One may perhaps reply that my remarks betray « signs of a sentimental attachment to everything that bears the seal of Tradition. » But is not « sentimentality » just as much — indeed more — involved in the desire for a very personal prayer « in which the words say exactly what I am feeling at this moment » ? Here too an excessive tendency to absolutize risks depriving the charismatic renewal of the fruit it is capable of bearing when it is properly understood and lived.

There is yet another temptation that besets certain passionate followers of the movement. At a time when the Church is striving with mankind to achieve greater justice and liberation for the oppressed masses, the charismatic renewal lays stress on a spiritual experience which, though closely connected with the common expression and the solidarity of the group, basically remains confined to the individual. The God of our faith seems to be associated mainly with religious « consolation, » in the positive and traditional sense. The mission of transforming this earth to make it worthy of man and more in keeping with God's creative purpose thus becomes so secondary that when one listens to or reads certain representatives of the movement, including some of its most distinguished members, one has the impression that it is a purely optional mission. To assemble a flock of praying figures is not the central task of the Christian mission. It would be unjust to disregard the importance which these groups attach to compassion, brotherly concern and the desire to relieve extreme poverty. The unselfish devotion of some members of the charismatic communities is a sharp lesson to our egoistic ways of living the Gospel. Their love, manifested in their relationships with the people they encounter or who seek their help, is often of such a quality that one is bound to admire it. Just as their fellowship and mutual caring represent a genuine return to the truth of Christian *koinonia*. But, generally speaking, they too readily confine themselves to the level of wounds to be dressed and afflictions to be healed, without proceeding to action. And all this takes place in a too unilaterally religious atmosphere of which a sign, among others, is the too uncritical emphasis on the rites of healing. While recognizing that there is a

wide variety of calls in the Body of Christ, one cannot
but regret that the concern to get down to the very root
of the evils which beset man in our modern societies by
working for the advent of a new humanity is so rarely present, and that the charismatics are so unwilling to be
challenged on this point. Especially when the persons involved are religious or nuns belonging to congregations
whose « secondary aim » is ministering to the poor.

*
* *

In short, the entry of religious into the charismatic
renewal is a phenomenon that theology must reflect upon.
I am by no means suggesting that the renewal as such is to
be avoided. For not only is it a sign of God's Spirit acting
in his People, but it has borne positive fruits for which
we are thankful. Christian communities that once vege-
tated in a dismal search for the state of grace — just as
much as is needed to go to heaven —have been revitalized
by the renewal. People tormented by difficult and, at
first sight, unsolvable problems have received from their
charismatic group the brotherly help that has enabled them
to face the future hopefully. An increasing number of
young men and women are hearing, in the experience
they are living, a call to commit themselves unreservedly to
the service of the Gospel. And others, previously caught in
a kind of anonymous Christianity, are relearning to spread
the Good News around them. All this is positive, and many
religious communities slumbering in a pious mediocrity
and incapable of healing their own divisions, would doubtless benefit by breathing in a gust of this bracing evangelical

fresh air which would awaken them from their slumber.

But on one condition : this charismatic inspiration must be integrated with what is specific and fundamental to their vocation and already makes that vocation — independently of any entry into the charismatic renewal — a genuinely « charismatic » one, in the broad sense that I defined earlier. Such an assertion may seem banal, but it is pregnant with implications.

In the first place, it is obvious that the manifestations and activities in which the charismatic renewal is incarnated can only be *means* serving the specific type of evangelical life that the « following of Christ » demands in this or that religious family. They cannot become the supreme activity, the end sought for its own sake. And this applies even to contemplative or monastic religious vocations. The *lectio divina,* the choral celebration of the divine office, must find in these activities not a substitute but an aid and a support. The nuance is of capital importance, but in certain « testimonies » that I have read, I am surprised to find enthusiastic assertions that totally diregard it. In the case of religious consecrated to the apostolic life, the same holds true of the missionary commitments in which they realize the particular charism of their congregation or order.

Need I stress how important it is not to let oneself be carried away by excessive and extravagant forms of the charismatic élan ? Like the enthusiasm for penance and other forms of popular religiosity which at certain periods invaded the spirituality of the orders or congregations, prophecy, ecstatic attitudes, inspired gestures, doubtful manifestations of glossolalia can ruin the *koinonia* if they are not kept under control. And often they make the religious life rather ridiculous. Today we are amused by the Stylites on their high pillars, the Dendrites, the rock-dwelling saints and all the excesses of the Syrian ascetics. Perhaps we will also laugh, in a not too distant future, at the inspired meetings where the participants wait for the Spirit to manifest his perceptible presence. And the account of the provincial superior accepting as a line of conduct what a Sister with the gift of prophecy « declares in the Spirit » at a prayer meeting will be filed in the museum of unusual phenomena. Ridicule kills, and today it is so essential for the religious life to regain its health that it cannot lay itself open to ridicule.

There is another very important point to be considered. Despite official protests, the charismatic renewal glosses over and sometimes relegates to a very unworthy background the need for serious reflection on the objective content of revelation. Some of its followers appear to be satisfied with a series of biblical sayings that are interpreted according to the sentiment they awaken in the speaker. Now the various religious traditions of the « following of Christ » have always — and rightly — emphasized the necessity of discovering, contemplating and proclaiming what God has said of himself « once for all » (*ephapax*) in his Son, independently of what I may feel and experience in my own spiritual adventure. The danger of romanticizing the Word (the obverse of a lack of spiritual poverty) does threaten certain communities. To be aware of it, one has only to assist at what is called « a sharing of Scripture. » It is therefore a problem to be taken very seriously. Far more seriously than we do in fact. Pietism and fundamentalism can take many forms, but all are pitfalls. The fact that a practice « does

some good » is not enough to establish it as *the* practice to
be followed. How can one fail to be astonished at the lack
of clear thinking that is evidenced in this domain ? How
can one fail to feel profoundly saddened when one hears
a group of contemplatives trying to express « what the
Spirit is saying to them » by citing this or that text of
Paul, but in a faulty translation whose errors they could
have avoided simply by consulting a good commentary. It
is not sufficiently appreciated that the Spirit who speaks
in our hearts is the very one who inspired the Scriptures,
and that these, understood according to their obvious
meaning, are the norms of the Christian faith and spiritual experience.

Finally, let us note a danger of which several congregations are themselves becoming aware. Those who have
received « baptism in the Spirit » are often tempted to
regard themselves as an inner circle of « truly spiritual »
men and women. Although spiritual experiences of every
kind can be but *a* sign of the Spirit, they unconsciously
tend to make them *the* sign of the Spirit, the sign that
enables them to recognize the small sect of authentic
Christians. In so doing, they forget that the Sermon on
the Mount vigorously asserts :

> On that day many will say to me, « Lord, Lord, did we not pro-
> phesy in your name, and cast out demons in your name, and
> do many mighty works in your name ? » And then will I
> declare to them, « I never knew you ; depart from me, you
> evildoers » (Mt 7, 22-23).

For every sign of the Spirit reveals its source only
through the love that accompanies it. In his first Letter to
the Corinthians (1 Co 13), Paul is careful to point out
that the Christian criterion in this domain is neither the

quantity nor the extraordinariness of the individual or collective experience, but the quality of the love of God and mankind that surrounds the experience. Supernatural gifts and spiritual phenomena cannot be called Christian unless they actualize our love for God and our neighbours. For the gift of the Spirit must enable people to encounter not a charismatic but the Lord through that charismatic. [9] That is the real criterion. The charism has to transcend the level of experience confined to the person or the group — including all the joy and peace one may derive from it — and lead on to the service of the Lord's glory. The gifts of the Spirit are not primarily ecstatic but doxological. They are not primarily a privilege but a service (1 Co 12, 5-7). The desire to praise and serve is the very opposite of exclusiveness. Hence one must necessarily feel disturbed when one sees individuals forming in-groups that are more fascinated by the ecstatic experience than by love. For when coteries are born in a community, when the followers of the « renewal » are so touchy that they sense an attack in every objective criticism, one is entitled to suspect that it is not the Lord's Spirit who is at work there. No attitude that erodes *koinonia,* fellowship — the essential fruit of the Spirit in the « following of Christ » project — can come from that Spirit of God.

Therefore if the « charismatic renewal » is a sign of the action of God's Spirit at this turning-point in the history of his People — and I believe that it must be acknowledged as such — then the time has come for us to look at its manifestations in a more searching and critical fash-

---

9. As A. BITTLINGER emphasizes in his book *Gifts and Graces,* London, 1967, pp. 80-81.

ion. After the liturgical renewal and its arid moments a
door has finally been left ajar, and through it have rushed
all the desires for marvels, for free religious expression,
for spiritual enthusiasm which slumber in the human
heart. But it is of the utmost importance to check all the
findings, not in order to « quench the Spirit » but, on the
contrary, to keep his flame alive. Let us look squarely at
the facts in order to retain what is good, to dismiss what
is useless or harmful, and to avoid making this or that
aspect of spiritual experience the be-all and the end-all of
Christianity. Paul said as much to the Thessalonians :

> Never try to quench the Spirit or treat the gift of prophecy
> with contempt ; think before you do anything — hold on to
> what is good and avoid every form of evil. (I Th. 5, 19-22) [10]

This applies particularly to the religious and nuns who
are attracted by the present forms of the charismatic renewal. It would be foolish just to advise them to « shun
that temptation » : if the gifts of the Spirit are so many
forces that are meant to build up the Kingdom of God, the
religious who receives them must welcome them as a grace
and endeavour to integrate them with that great charism
which is his call from Christ. But it would be equally
senseless to encourage those religious to throw themselves
blindly and indiscriminately into excesses that are thought

---

10. At this point TOB provides the following commentary : « Here
we already have, in rough outline, the rules that Paul will give to
the church of Corinth in order to foster in the Christian community
a truly positive attitude towards the manifestations of the Spirit. These
gifts have to be respected, but they are not the be-all and end-all of
Christianity. Moreover, Christians have to ' discern the spirits ' in
order to distinguish between what is good and what is useless » (p.
625, note g).

to be inspired by the Spirit but endanger their own form of vocation, which is profoundly charismatic. The extraordinary gifts of the Spirit must be woven into the fabric of the basic charism which, in their case, is the « following of Christ. » Is there not a hierarchy in the charismatic universe (understood in the broader sense) ? And does not this hierarchy call for balance ?

I therefore believe that it is necessary to reflect deeply on the charismatic nature of the religious project. Such a reflection is the only one that can help religious to see where they stand in relation to the charismatic renewal and to discover their own way of fitting into it if they believe it can benefit them. It is the only reflection that makes possible the search for the religious identity, beyond the barrier of mistrust and sterile polemics. There is no question here of being « for » or « against » this or that spiritual experience or miraculous manifestation or form of popular religiosity. What matters is to understand how all these activities and attitudes can be consonant with the ways of God and with the basic call to « follow Christ » on the path of his Sovereignty. To put it bluntly : certain charismatic excesses might prevent religious from fully grasping and living the demand « follow Me. » And Christ's « follow Me » does in fact resound in the summons to empty oneself : it lies at the heart of that summons. Now, as Paul's hymn in the Letter to the Philippians makes clear, that self-emptying requires the nakedness of an utterly humble faith. When God manifests his presence, he has to be welcomed. But when we search too eagerly for signs of his power and have too great a yearning for wonderful signs that gratify our sensibility to the full, are we not implicitly rejecting the desert ? Certainly, faith and religion call to each other, but the consolations of religion, unless kept under control, risk obscuring faith's secret affinity with the Cross of the Servant. [11] The great experience of life in the Spirit is encountered more on the arid, bumpy path of faith than on the path of glossolalias, prophecies, baptisms in the Spirit and healings, which the charismatic renewal often tends to favour.

---

11. This point is well brought out by a member of the Renewal : J. Cl. CAILLAUX, *Un sourire de Dieu, chemin à travers le Renouveau charismatique*, Paris, 1976. But one cannot help wondering whether his perceptive analysis really ties up with the content of current « charismatic » literature, especially in the magazines where members of the Renewal spontaneously express their conviction.

I

It is difficult for a religious to say straightaway what brought him or her to the « following of Christ. » Indeed, the most immediate reasons for entering the religious life may conceal an implicit and more profound motivation that becomes explicit when one examines them more closely. Those immediate reasons vary according to persons, circumstances and epochs. One knocks on the door of a novitiate because one is attracted by the community's specific work, by the importance it attaches to the contemplative dimension of Christianity, or by the evangelical quality of life found within its walls. All these reasons enter into the choice of this form of Christian living ; but those who are satisfied with them and do not look for the deeper motivation risk never getting down to the essentials. In the circumstances they may simply persevere in the religious life without living it as a profoundly meaningful experience.

Beyond the Purely Moral Motivations

To get to the truth of the religious life, we must obviously discover its central pivot. But the latter will not
stand out in bold relief unless we look at it from another
standpoint than that of usefulness or moral value. And
it will not disclose itself as if by magic if we simply
qualify « usefulness » by adding « apostolic, » « evangelical, » or more explicitly, « in order to advance on the
path of perfection. »

Let us therefore admit that, to get to this truth, we have
a steep hill to climb. The understanding of the religious
project has been dominated by moral categories, especially since the emergence of what are commonly known
as the « active Orders » and the « apostolic congregations. » The community's secondary aim (an inadequate
expression but one that will be more familiar to the reader) has become the priority aim. Councils, popes and
bishops have been led by circumstances to regard the
great variety of congregations mainly — if not almost
exclusively — as a providential source of apostolic man-
power generously placed at the service of the Christian
mission.

From this standpoint, it is fascinating to study the
discussions held by Vatican II when it was preparing
the decree *Perfectae caritatis* : they are more preoccupied
with Martha's vocation than with Mary's, and they stress
the necessity of « finding God, *but in the works of the*

apostolic life. » [1] Moreover, the *aggiornamento* chapters have readily embraced this point of view. It would be no exaggeration to say that the intense « *missionary* » mobilization, supported by verbal exhortations, that characterized the life of the postconciliar Church was predominant in the religious orders. [2] There is no need to labour this point. So I shall simply add that the prestigious adjective « missionary » enabled the religious life to regild its coat of arms : it was a « useful » life ; one was a religious *in order to* serve the Church and the world genuinely. Thus the religious life could give new splendour to its ancient reputation.

This phenomenon is not specific to the post-conciliar period. When one reads the little pamphlets formerly issued by the congregations to recruit new members, one is struck by the fact that everything revolved around two moral themes : apostolic commitment and personal sanctification. And this outlook was not confined to the Roman Catholic Church. When in the Anglican Communion, for example, the religious orders began to flourish again, it was because of their « usefulness » that they were finally accepted by the episcopal body. [3] P.F. Anson, who tells us that the bishops regarded the Sisters as a group of unmarried persons living together *to consecrate themselves to the ser-*

1. See J.M.R. TILLARD and Y. CONGAR, *L'adaptation et la rénovation de la vie religieuse, Unam Sanctam* series, No. 62, Paris, 1967, 234-235.

2. For this missionary mobilization, see the study by P. JACQUEMONT, J.P. JOSSUA and B. QUELQUEJEU, *Le temps de la patience, étude sur le témoignage,* Paris, 1976, especially 5-20 (69).

3. See M. HILL's excellent remarks in *The Religious Order. A Study of Virtuous Religion and Its Legitimation in the Nineteenth-Century Church of England,* London, 1973, 167-183.

vice of charity,[4] reveals a state of mind that was everywhere prevalent. From this standpoint we may even ask
ourselves whether the diaconate has not to a large extent
swallowed up the religious vocation. The problem becomes acute when lay religious, and especially lay sisters,
begin to manifest the desire to be entrusted with ecclesial
ministries. For there can be little doubt that among the
clerical religious (with the possible exception of the
monks) the priesthood has usually taken precedence over
the specific elements of religious profession. Many personal crises have sprung from the awareness that one's entire life had become but an existence *for, in order to...* A
for explained solely by the « moral » requirements of
generosity, the service of mankind and endless devotion.
In short, an existence which, deprived of the activity that
used to fill it in former days, was losing its significance.

The reader may object that the universally present
themes of personal sanctification and the search for perfection help to balance this too heavy emphasis on practical utility. And he might add — as most Christians would
today — that this sanctification can and must be achieved
not concurrently with apostolic action but as part of it,
for all dichotomies are to be avoided. One of the graces
of our time is precisely the rediscovery of the sanctifying
value of action undertaken for the Gospel. By serving man
in caritate, one enters into existential communion with
Jesus Christ. In the midst of action, the Christian's gaze
can reach, through mankind, to the fountain of love that
springs from the heart of God.

---

4. P.F. ANSON, *The Benedictines of Caldey,* London, 1940,
XVII (this work is cited by M. HILL, 168).

Granted all this, the fact remains that the striving for personal sanctification, even when it is closely bound up with the evangelical service of mankind, is a moral process. It is an effort man makes, under the action of grace, to realize his true human stature. Does not the religious maintain that fidelity to the internal dynamics of his project is a *means of* becoming (an *in order to*) what God wishes him to become ? In this light the religious life emerges as a school of perfection. Nothing can be more true, more specific to its nature. But does one enter the religious life primarily, basically, *in order to* find a school of perfection, a « school of service of the Lord » (Benedict) — or does one desire to find that *schola* of evangelical perfection and service because of another reason, which is perhaps less immediate, less explicit, but far deeper ? That is the question. And it is a crucial one.

Some may reply that, on the contrary, it is an idle question. In support of their argument they may point out that the great Rules are precisely a set of prescriptions and practical directions aiming to guide towards the perfection of charity those men and women who decided one day to follow Christ. The most obvious example of this is the Rule of St. Benedict where everything is drawn up in relation to the *dominici schola servitii* of which the Prologue speaks. [5] Within the monastery the members learn to hold their hearts and their bodies « ready to serve under holy obedience due to the precepts, » [6] thus achieving « what will be of lasting profit, » [7] patiently sharing the sufferings

---

5. *Prol.*, 45. In A. de VOGUE edition, *La Règle de Saint Benoît,* T. 1, coll. SC 181, Paris, 1972, 422 and 423.

6. *Prol.*, 40 ; *ibid.*, 422 and 423.

7. *Prol.*, 44 ; *ibid.*, 422 and 423.

of Christ « so that we may deserve to find a place in his Kingdom (*ut et Regno ejus mereamur esse consortes*). » [8] To this end the Rule enumerates the « instruments of the spiritual art (*instrumenta artis spiritualis*). » [9] One of the most insightful experts on the text and its sources com‑ ments : « The *ars sancta* is therefore meant to be a précis of Christian ethics for the use of the master and his pu‑ pils. » [10] And that is how it is presented both in the Rule of Benedict and in the anonymous *Rule of the Master* (c. 540) which Benedict used as a source. It is therefore not surprising to find in the middle of a contemporary study of the monastic renewal this spontaneous remark by the author, himself a monk :

> They (the present‑day cenobites) wish to be specialists in the Gospel alone. If they pray, it is because Christ asks all his faithful followers to pray. If they do penance, it is because Christ asks all his disciples to be converted. They wish to be contemplatives because there is no Christian holiness without contemplation. But they equally desire to be active, for there is no Christian holiness without action (...) They simply wish to be Christians. [11]

There is nothing unusual about this. The sole aim of every religious Rule is to prescribe the conduct that har‑ monizes with the freely chosen ideal. Essentially, the Rule is practical. And the more practical it is, the better it is. The Rule is not supposed to specify nor to present the spiritual experience that impels a Christian to choose this life style rather than another. This is very apparent in the history

---

8. *Prol.*, 50 ; *ibid.*, 424‑425. See also IV, 75‑77 ; *ibid.*, 462‑465.
9. IV, 75 ; 462‑463.
10. A. de VOGUE, *La Règle...*, T. 4, coll. SC 184, 126.
11. B. BESRET, « Pour un renouveau du monachisme, » in *Etudes*, 326, 1967, 545‑562 (554).

of those wonderful, highly inspired spiritual writings known as the Rules of St Francis : shortly after the death of the *Poverello*, the Franciscans found it necessary to have more precise and concrete directions, since it was becoming impossible to interpret the Rule literally. Every Rule outlines a mode of life. It is not to be confused with a hymn to the Spirit who awakened a vocation. Hence whatever some of the more imaginative commentators of Benedict's Rule may say to the contrary, one does not become a religious *in order to* follow a Rule. A Christian follows a Rule because he perceives therein the guide that helps him to respond generously to a mysterious desire born of a particular experience of Christ and his Spirit. Through the Rule he enters on a path of virtue, asceticism and moral conduct. This is necessary. But the Rule and the life style which it makes possible are there to serve a wholly different area of the Christian existence. Not the area of moral conduct, action, merit and perfection, but that of the experience of God, of a God-centred and of — at last I venture to say it ! — a charismatic experience.

A *Charismatic Call and Project*

In terms of its deepest source, the religious project is of the charismatic order, although the religious may not be aware of this from the start, but only after reviewing his life. What do I mean by « charismatic » in this context ? I mean that it is the Spirit alone who takes the initiative in the experience that leads a Christian to choose this type

of life, and also that such an experience lies beyond the
rational. That Christian finds himself in a climate closely
resembling that of the poetic experience, in which the
human mind feels possessed by what the ancients called a
daimon (demon) who inspires it by raising it above its
own limitations.

At the religious level we then speak of enthusiasm. [12]
And here we observe that, like artistic enthusiasm — which
has been compared to an intoxication that carries man far
away from the rational and the normal — religious enthusiasm, if not kept under control, can lead to the worst
excesses. It often goes hand in hand with fanaticism and
all kinds of illuminism. Sometimes it borders on madness.
But the fact remains that when religious enthusiasm is
rooted in an authentic experience of the divine, it is the
mainspring of those bursts of inspiration which restore to
mankind its sense of the transcendent and its thirst for
God. As James Dunn notes, the birth of the Church, under
the breath of Pentecost, is presented to us in the Acts as
the emergence of « an enthusiastic sect within first-century
Judaism. » [13] And he goes on to say :

> If any event can be described as the birthday of Christianity,
> it is the event which probably took place on the first Pentecost

---

12. On religious enthusiasm, see H. LEWY, *Sobria ebrietas :
untersuchungen zur Geschichte der antiken Mystik*, Giessen, 1929 ;
A. DELATTE, *Les conceptions de l'enthousiasme chez les philosophes
présocratiques*, Paris, 1934 ; R.A. KNOX, *Enthusiasm : a Chapter in
the History of Religion*, Oxford, 1950 ; G. SCHRENK, « Geist und
Enthusiasmus, » in *Studien zu Paulus*, Zurich, 1954, 107-127 ; O.
KUSS, « Enthusiasmus und Realismus bei Paulus », in *Auslegung
und Verkündigung*, I, Regensburg, 1963, 260-270.
13. The expression is used by James D. G. DUNN, *Jesus and
the Spirit*, « New Testament Library » series, London, 1975, 157.

following Jesus' death and initial resurrection appearances. On that day a gathering of Jesus' disciples, in a state, it would appear, of some eschatological excitement, enjoyed an experience of such spiritual power that they could only conclude that the Spirit of God had been bestowed upon them in eschatological measure. The experience should neither be reduced to nor seen solely in terms of its phenomena, ecstatic vision and glossolalia. For those involved, so far as we can tell, these latter were only the concomitant circumstances of the invasion of divine power from without — a natural human expression of and reaction to the encounter with the divine. This initial experience of being filled with power from God was repeated not infrequently at individual or group level (Acts 4, 8, 31 ; 8, 17f ; 9, 17 ; 10, 44ff ; 13, 9 ; 19, 6 ; cf. Eph. 5, 18).

The enthusiasm which resulted from these experiences was a powerful force binding those involved in close fellowship (...) In other words, the earliest Christian community was essentially charismatic and enthusiastic in nature, in every aspect of its common life and worship, its development and mission. [14]

In the enthusiasm born of an experience of the Spirit we therefore have to distinguish two levels of depth. The first is wholly personal and inward : the person experiences God's power filling him, he feels that he is being seized by the Spirit and urged to place his living strength under the power of the Spirit. The second is more external : this encounter with the Spirit is expressed in a wide range of phenomena and gestures which are not in themselves typically evangelical but belong to mankind's ancient religious heritage. For — and the experts agree on this point — glossolalia, prophecy, ecstasy, thaumaturgy, the gift of healing are found in all religions. [15] And this is

---

14. *Ibid.*, 193-194.
15. On this point, see especially J. P. KILDAHL, *The Psychology of Speaking in Tongues*, New York - Evanston - San Francisco - London, 1972 ; M. L. CARLYLE, A *Survey of Glossolalia and Re-*

so undeniable that, before reminding us that charismatic phenomena were as prevalent outside the Christian communities as in the Pauline churches, James Dunn, one of the scholars who most readily acknowledge the place of « marvels » in the New Testament writings, states that « for Paul there is nothing distinctively Christian in charismatic phenomena as such. » [16] And he enlarges on this statement :

> When we set early Christianity in the context of its times, the full ambiguity of the charismata becomes apparent (...) This does not mean that charismata cease to be important within the Pauline community. Not at all ! (...) : the ambiguity of the manifestation of the divine does not make that manifestation any less essential to spiritual and community life. What our conclusion means is this : (1) charismata in themselves could not be taken as a mark of specifically Christian experience or of a higher stage of experience within Christianity (against the Corinthian gnostics) or of special commission as a servant of Christ (against the Corinthian « false apostles »). In other words, the *danger* of charismatic experience and the need for *controls* on charismata within the Christian community is confirmed and underlined. (2) Since charismatic experience as

---

lated Phenomena in Non-Christian Religions, in American Anthropologist 58, 1956, 75-96 ; A. GODIN, « Moi perdu ou Moi retrouvé dans l'expérience charismatique : perplexité des psychologues, » in Actes de la XIIᵉ Conférence Internationale de sociologie religieuse, Rapport nᵒ 14, 309-335 ; F. D. GOODMAN et al., Speaking in Tongues, a Cross-Cultural Study, London-Chicago, 1972 ; James D.G. DUNN, op. cit., 302-307 (a remarkable synthesis of the field of these phenomena in the time of Christ) ; F. KONIG, « Glossolalia, » in Diccionario de las religiones, Barcelona, 1964, 591-593 ; Robert M. GRANT, Miracle and Natural Law in Graeco-Roman and Early Christian Thought, Amsterdam, 1962. A few brief allusions in W. G. KUMMEL, The Theology of the New Testament According to Its Major Witnesses, Jesus, Paul and John, « New Testament Library » series, London, 1974, 61.

16. James D.G. DUNN, op. cit., 302. Same assertion ibid., 307.

such does not bring us to the heart of distinctively Christian experience for Paul, we must dig more deeply and pursue our quest into other aspects of Paul's religious experience. [17]

This elucidation is of prime importance. For just as the charismatic phenomena which translated the primitive community's enthusiasm born of the Spirit belong to man-kind's ancient religious heritage, so too does the monastic life (and the other forms of religious life which in one way or another derive from it) continue an old religious tradition which is found outside Christianity. The monas-tic phenomenon is one of the constants of the great reli-gions. It has its own consistency, which explains the present-day endeavours to bring about an encounter between the different forms of monachism throughout the world. [18] I

---

17. Ibid., 307.
18. Among the numerous works on this theme, see especially : « Les moines bouddhistes et hindous, » special issue of Collectanea Cisterciencia 29, 1967, 129-194 (articles by Louis MERTON and Francis MAHIEU ; report by Louis MERTON) ; SUKUMAR DUTT, Early Buddhist Monachism, London, 1960 (2nd ed.) ; Augustin HIDESHI KISHI, Spiritual Consciousness in Zen from a Thomistic Theological Point of View, « Theologia Montis Regis » series 46, Montreal, 1966 ; « Bangkok, rencontre des moines d'Asie, » special issue of Rythmes du monde, 42, 1968 ; A. HEISING, « Benedik-tinisches Mönchtum und Biblische Botschaft, » in Liturgie und Mönchtum, Laacher Hefts, Heft 43, 1968, 13-19 ; S. LASSIER, « Le renoncement en Inde, » in Christus 66, 1970, 249-258 ; E. CORNELIS, « Phénomène universel de la vie religieuse, » in Lumière et Vie 96, 1970, 4-24 ; J. LECLERCQ, Le défi de la vie contemplative, ch. 1, Paris, 1970 ; ID., Vie religieuse et vie contemplative, Paris, 1970, 207-264 ; ID., Moines et moniales ont-ils un avenir, Brussels, 1971, 173-179 ; ID., « Le monachisme comme phénomène mondial, » in Vie Spir. Suppl., 1973, 461-478 ; E. PEZET, « Le monachisme bouddhique ; un défi séculaire aux traditions spirituelles de la chrétienté, » in Irénikon 48, 1975, 5-40 ; in collaboration, Les

shall return to this point later. But it is already clear that
when the monastic life became incorporated into Christianity, it necessarily depended on and expressed what is
genuinely and specifically Christian. For just as the Christian community has its « false prophets, » who must be
rejected « no matter how inspired, how charismatic they
seem to be, » [19] and glossolalists so inflated and overexcited
that, in his time, Paul had to bring those of Corinth to
their senses, [20] aberrant forms of the religious life can also
spring up in the Churches. Like all the realities of the
natural religious universe, monachism and its derivative
or kindred forms have to be evangelized in order to become fully Christian. Without that evangelization and
baptism, they do have their own value — an important
one, consistent with the Gospel — as a school of moral
conduct, a way of perfection, a guide to the ascetic life
and an initiation on contemplation, but they do not have
that extra quality which makes them specifically Christian.
In extreme cases they may even exhibit traces of phari-
saism, by which I mean an excessive trust in the value of
human efforts or self-satisfaction at the thought of the
merits one is sure to acquire. Obtrusive glossolalia, false

---

moines chrétiens face aux religions d'Asie ; *Bangalore 1973,* Vanves,
1974 (in English in *Cistercian Studies* 1974 and 1975).

19. James D.G. DUNN, *op. cit.,* 296.

20. The exegesis of 1 Co 14, 20-25 becomes clearer « if we assume
that the passage is polemically directed against those in Corinth who
regard speaking in tongues too highly. As the form of V. 22 suggests,
this faction have maintained that glossolalia is a sign for believers,
that it is a proof of pneumatic status and authority. Paul refutes
this » (James D.G. DUNN, *ibid.,* 230, who takes up the position
of J. P. M. SWEET, « A Sign for Unbelievers : Paul's Attitude to
Glossolalia, » in *NTS* 13, 1966-1967, 240-246).

prophecies, questionable healings, ambiguous ecstasies bear much the same relation to the « wonders and marvels » aspect of religion (especially in its popular expression) as do harsh moralisms, blundering pharisaisms and abso- lute asceticisms to its ethical aspect.

What, then, is the experience of evangelical enthusiasm in which the religious project must necessarily be grounded to be genuinely charismatic ? It is an experience of faith, in the strict sense of the word.

To discover the content of this experience, we have to scrutinize the Gospel. In a previous study I have shown how the religious project carried on, as it were, the « fol- lowing of Christ » of the apostles. Now all the New Tes- tament accounts of personal vocations have common traits, and when these are singled out they are most revealing.

The most striking and possibly the most essential of those traits is that the chosen person does not ask to be chosen, he is not seeking to fulfil his personal quest for perfection — indeed the vocation of the rich young man, which would seem to fit this description, comes to nothing (Mt 19, 16-30 ; Mk 10, 17-31 ; Lk 18, 18-30). Rather it is Jesus himself who, in one way or another, issues the invitation. Admittedly, John lays less emphasis on the Master's will spontaneously bursting forth in the everyday life of the chosen one (Jn 1, 35-51), and the followers would appear to come to Jesus less directly : it is because they have heard John the Baptist, whose disciples they are, that Andrew and his companion feel urged to follow Jesus (1, 37-38) ; Andrew's enthusiastic testimony leads Simon to Jesus (1, 42), and Philip's has the same effect on Nathanael (1, 45-46). But we must note, on the other hand, that Philip's vocation (1, 43) can only be explained

by Jesus' direct invitation. [21] And the author of chapter
21, appended to the body of the fourth gospel, shows
Simon Peter's vocation to be wholly dependent on the
Lord's « follow me ! » (21, 19, 22). [22] In accordance with
his usual method, John is probably rereading the « vocations » traditions in the light of his theological aim. As
Raymond E. Brown points out,

> John has placed on the lips of the disciples at this moment
> a synopsis of the gradual increase of understanding that took
> place throughout the ministry of Jesus and after the resur-
> rection. John has used the occasion of the call of the disciples
> to summarize discipleship in its whole development. [23]

The accounts of the calling of Paul, the last of the
Apostles, present many difficult problems to exegesis because of their marked discrepancies. One thing, however,
is clear : it is emphasized that Paul was a sinner, persecu-
ting Christ in his brethren (Acts 9, 4-5 ; 22, 7-8 ; 26, 14-
15), and seeking to destroy the Church (Gal 1, 13), when
the Lord seized hold of him and gave him his vocation.
Therefore, if in the years following the Resurrection the
« following of Christ » no longer exhibited the traits it
bore when the disciples accompanied Jesus in his travels
and stayed constantly by his side, the same fundamental
law nonetheless obtains. It is Christ who takes the initiative. He suddenly invades the life of a person who is not
necessarily better than other men and may even be a noto-

---

21. This is underlined by R. SCHNACKENBURG, *The Gospel
according to St John,* vol. 1, Montreal, 1968, 313.

22. See C. K. BARRETT, *The Gospel according to St John,*
London, 1962, 487.

23. Raymond E. BROWN, *The Gospel according to St John I-XII,*
London, Chapman, 1971, 78.

rious sinner. Such an encounter is determinative for the life of that person. It challenges the whole of his being, and this questioning leads on, in one way or another, to the service of the Kingdom. And it is only through his Spirit that the risen Lord thus intervenes. If we all agree that the word « charism » signifies an activity of the Spirit and not of man, that it is a humanly perceptible manifestation of God's grace, a gift presupposing no previous merit on the part of the receiver, the experience of being seized by the Lord's power, the consciousness of thus entering into the mysterious economy of the eschatological times, [24] then we must admit that the calling of the apostles — including Paul's vocation — can be understood only in the perspective of God's charismatic realm.

Here, too, Christ's demand has the extra-ordinary, abnormal and irrational traits which characterize the irruption of the world of the Spirit. For, taken together, the gospel passages which allude to this call translate an almost impracticable demand : « Immediately they left their nets and followed him » (Mt 4, 20 ; Mk 1, 18) ; « He called them. Immediately they left the boat and their father and followed him » (Mt 4, 22 ; Mk 1, 20) ; « He said to him, ' Follow me. ' And he left everything, and rose and followed him » (Lk 5, 28) ; « Another of the disciples said to him, ' Lord, let me first go and bury my father. ' But Jesus said to him, ' Follow me, and leave the dead to bury their dead ' » (Mt 8, 22 ; Lk 9, 59-60); « Go,

---

24. See James D.G. DUNN's summary of Paul's views in *op. cit.*, 253-258. See also G. HASENHUETTL, *Charisma : Ordnungsprinzip der Kirche*, Herder, 1969, 235-238 ; H. SCHUERMANN, « Les charismes spirituels, » in *L'Eglise de Vatican II*, » Unam Sanctam » series 51 b, Paris, 1966, 541-573.

sell what you have, and give to the poor, and you will
have treasure in heaven ; then come, follow me » (Mk
10, 21 ; Mt 19, 21 ; Lk 18, 22) ; « We have left everything and followed you » (Mt 19, 27) ; « There is no
man who has left house or wife or brothers or parents or
children, for the sake of the kingdom of God, who will
not receive... » (Lk 18, 29 ; Mt 19, 29 ; Mk 10, 29) ;
« For his sake I have suffered the loss of all things » (Ph
3, 8). While history follows its course, the chosen one
must let himself be penetrated by the Spirit of the « last
times, » the eschatological times — time has already
« hauled up its sails» (1 Co 7, 29) — and he is asked to
accept the logic of this situation, without making com-
promises. The climate is that of chapter 7 of *I Corinthians,*
where Paul speaks of virginity and, in a broader sense, of
the situation of the *agamoi,* those who have no spouse
(bachelors, widowers, husbands separated from their
wives, young men about to get married). [25] Since the time
is nigh when God will be « all in all » — Paul believes
that the Parousia is near (1 Co 15, 51-53) — why not,
while anticipating the Parousia, « deal with the world as
though one had no dealings with it » (1 Co 7, 31) ?

In the apostolic call it is the Lord himself, through his
Spirit, who thus alerts man to the reality of the last times,
asking him to live as a « witness » to the Gospel's great
assertion : the Kingdom of God is *already* at the door,
and to stress that it is bursting in by rising above the
horizontal line of history and the usual way men fulfil
their destiny. The fullness of the Spirit of « the last times, »

25. On celibacy regarded as a charism, see James D.G. DUNN,
op. cit., 206-207, 256.

which the charismatic outpourings of Pentecost manifest on the plane of perceptible phenomena with their « miraculous » aura (« they are full of new wine », Ac 2, 13), is translated here to the plane of life itself and its essential dynamics. Man is affected in the root of his desire. The apostolic call is charismatic, if it is true that the fundamental charism of every Christian life is precisely the perception « in the Holy Spirit » of a wish of God becoming the motive force of one's existence [26] and impressing its demands on that existence.

When the religious life was subsequently born in the Church (at a fairly early date it seems), it wished to link up with this experience of the apostolic call. In a previous study I have assembled and analysed testimonies showing that its followers were immediately aware of this. [27] Adopting a standpoint somewhat different from mine and using another vocabulary : that of the concept of *kairos* (a Greek word denoting the decisive moment when man's freedom is suddenly called in question [28]), Fr. E. Pousset, also describing the call of the apostles, writes :

> It is in such a « *kairos* » that a religious vocation is born, and it is in such a concept of time that it is grounded. It does not impose on the summoned one a stiffer dose of evangelical morality ; but it affects him here and now in the root of his being, leaving him no reasonable choice but to say Yes to the Kingdom of God, who needs him for a task and invests him

---

26. See *ibid.*, 222-225.
27. J.M.R. TILLARD, *Devant Dieu et pour le monde : le projet des religieux*, « Cogitatio fidei » series 75, Paris, 1974.
28. On the concept of *kairos*, see DELLING's article « Kairos, » in G. KITTEL, *TWNT*, T. 3, 455-464, especially 459-462). See also J.A.T. ROBINSON, *In the End God*, London, 1968, 44-55.

inwardly, in his life style, but without instantly renewing him
through and ,through in the depths of his spiritual being. It
follows that the summoned one is neither more saintly nor
more perfect than that other man whom the Lord has not called
away from his wife and children and the trade he usually pur-
sues at home, in Jericho, Bethany or Capernaum. [29]

If, as is fairly obvious, the religious vocation does not
of itself make the religious more morally perfect, just as
it does not crown a higher perfection, this is precisely because it belongs to another level of existence : that of
God's sudden and gratuitous invasion of a life, a bursting-
forth of God closely related with the hastening of the
Kingdom. [30] In short, the level of the Spirit.

A God - Centred Wonder :
A Decision « Because ,of Christ »

Since man's freedom is involved, it is clear that God's
call awakens in the believer an initial reaction which con-
stitutes the soil in which the decisions he has to take
(« leave everything ! ») will germinate. But this reaction
is not first and foremost of the moral, ethical and practical order : primarily it is one of enthusiasm. And in this
context enthusiasm is fundamentally doxological, adoring.

So far I have examined only the vocation narratives
found, not too frequently, in the New Testament. But

---

29. E. POUSSET, « Religieux et chrétiens dans le monde, »
in *Vie consacrée* 44, 1972, 65-96 (75).

30. See G. HASENHUETTL, *op. cit.*, 121-122.

there are other New Testament passages that shed light on man's attitude in the encounter with Christ which re-orients his life. The most important of these is the double parable of the treasure and the fine pearl (Mt 13, 44-46). Exegetes have noted, moreover, that the words describing the decision of the person who finds the treasure or the fine pearl « find a direct echo in Jesus' injunction to the rich young man : ' Go, and sell what you own and give the money to the poor, and you will have treasure in heaven ; then come, follow me '. » [31] This is the context of the apostolic call. [32] The texts do not compare the Kingdom as such to the treasure or the pearl : they com-pare *what happens within a man* discovering the Kingdom to what happens within a man finding the treasure or the pearl. [33] All this is highly relevant to our subject.

It would be wrong to maintain, especially by adducing the vocation narratives, that the point of these two par-ables is the command to make an absolute gift of all one's possessions to the poor, the summons to take an heroic decision. In other words, these parables do not primarily imply that whoever finds the Kingdom *must* leave every-thing and accept every sacrifice if he wishes to enter it. [34] In the episode of the rich young man, Matthew does, of

---

31. See J. DUPONT, « Les paraboles du trésor et de la perle, » in NTS 14, 1967-1968, 408-418 (415, 418) ; C.H. DODD, *The Parables of the Kingdom*, London, 1948, 112-113.

32. See C. H. DODD, *ibid.*, 113. Note the nuances of E. LIN-NEMANN, *Parables of Jesus*, London, 1966, 103 and 172-173 (note 16).

33. A point underlined especially by P. BONNARD, *L'évangile selon saint Matthieu*, Neuchâtel-Paris, 1963, 207. See also J. DUPONT, *art. cit.*, 413.

34. See E. LINNEMANN, *op. cit.*, 100 (with note h).

course, stress the necessity of giving up all one's possessions for the sake of the Kingdom. [35] There can be no half measures ! But here the key-idea would seem to be the following : it is self-evident that whoever discovers the Kingdom leaves everything in order to enter it. And « the fact that the man buys the field containing the treasure... signifies... that it is *worth while* relinquishing everything for the sake of this Kingdom. » [36] In both parables the relinquishment of which the Gospel speaks is important, but more as a result of discovering the Kingdom than as the steps one must take in order to enter it.

For the decision man takes at that moment, a radical decision, is « commensurate to his discovery » [37] and to the joy of his discovery. As Joachim Jeremias tells us :

> The key-words are « in his joy » (*apo tès charas* ; v. 44 : they are not expressly repeated in the case of the merchant, but they apply to him as well). When that great joy, beyond all measure, seizes a man, it carries him away, penetrates his inmost being, subjugates his mind. All else seems valueless compared with that surpassing worth ; no price is too high, and the unreserved surrender of what is most valuable becomes a matter of course. The decisive thing in the double parable is not what the two men give up, but the reason for their doing so : the overwhelming experience of the greatness of their discovery. So it is with the Kingdom of God. The effect of the joyful news is overpowering ; it fills the heart with gladness, making life's whole aim the consummation of the divine community, and producing the most whole-hearted self-sacrifice. [38]

---

35. This has been excellently brought out by S. LEGASSE, *L'appel du riche : contribution à l'étude des fondements scripturaires de l'état religieux*, Paris, 1966.

36. P. BONNARD, *op. cit.*, 207-208.

37. *Ibid.*, 207.

38. J. JEREMIAS, *Rediscovering the Parables*, London, SCM Press, 1963, 158.

The inestimable value of the Kingdom relegates every-thing else to the background. This does not mean that other goods and personal relationships are rejected or held in contempt, but rather that he who discovers the King-dom sees those other realities from the standpoint of his dependence on what has become the centre of his life. Consequently they cannot compete for his affection. Not because he has renounced them, but simply *because of* the attraction of the Kingdom and the joy it awakens. [39] It is in this light that we can understand the apparent inhumanity of assertions like : « If any one comes to me and does not hate his own father and mother and wife and children and brothers and sisters, yes, and even his own life, he cannot be my disciple » (Lk 14, 25). The mysterious enthusiasm created by the encounter with Jesus, coming into their lives at a decisive moment, can alone explain the action of Levi, leaving the customs-house to « follow him, » the decision of James and John, « leav-ing their father Zebedee in the boat with the hired ser-vants and following him » (Mk 1, 20), the attitude of Simon Peter, smitten with remorse and following him on the shore of the lake in order to be led where he would rather not go (Jn 21, 18).

The third chapter of the Letter to the Philippians has very different aspects but it places us in an analogous cli-mate. Whether or not Paul wrote the text — and in spite of F.C. Baur's doubts, its authenticity as a Pauline writing is nowadays increasingly accepted [40] — it clearly refers to

---

39. See J. M. R. TILLARD, *op. cit.*, 61-67. See also E. G. GULIN. *Die Freude im Neuen Testament*, Helsinki, 1932.

40. See F.W. BEARE, *The Epistle to the Philippians*, London,

Paul's state as a result of the Damascus road experience :
a state in which conversion and the apostolic call are intimately united. [41] The theme of joy runs through this
apparently disjointed letter and somehow links up its various parts (*1, 4, 18, 25 ; 2, 2, 17, 18, 28, 29 ; 3, 1 ; 4,
1, 4, 10*) ; joy constantly breaks through. It matters little
whether or not one half of Ph *3, 1* is the conclusion of the
previous chapter [42] : the context is wholly one of enthusiasm.

The joy to which I refer is joy *en kuriô*. Not simply a
joy whose object is Christ, but one that finds its whole
source and raison d'être in the dead and risen Christ,
« otherwise it would not be the unquestionably *trium-
phant* joy which resounds here. » [43] Moreover, it does not
spring from an experience of piety or inner delight,
but stands out against the background of a harrowing
situation which it transfigures. Because of this, « it is a
manifestation of the Spirit and one of the signs of God's
Reign. » [44] It is a realistic enthusiasm, if ever there was
one ; the enthusiasm associated not with a lighthearted,
youthful joy just brushing life with its wings, but with

1959, 1 ; J.F. COLLANGE, *L'Epître de saint Paul aux Philippiens*,
Neuchâtel-Paris, 1973, 20-21.

41. « The Damascus experience for Paul meant primarily his
commissioning to proclaim Jesus (as Son of God and Lord) to the
Gentiles » (James D.G. DUNN, *op. cit.*, 110).

42. See P. BONNARD, *L'Epître de saint Paul aux Philippiens*,
« Commentaire du Nouveau Testament » series X, Neuchâtel-Paris,
1950, 59-60 ; J. F. COLLANGE, *op. cit.*, 107.

43. K. BARTH, *Commentary on the Epistle to the Philippians*,
(1927). See P. BONNARD, *L'Epître de saint Paul...*, 59-60.

44. J. F. COLLANGE, *op. cit.*, p. 44, who refers to Rm *14, 17* ;
15, 13 ; Ga *5, 22* ; 1 Th *1, 6*.

a joy which — despite sufferings, failures and disappoint-
ments — springs from communion with the Lord Jesus.
The communion that faith engenders.

How does Paul describe this communion ? As « the
knowledge of Christ Jesus my Lord » (Ph 3, 7). With
such knowledge, all Paul hopes for is to become like Christ
in his death, and to share his sufferings while awaiting a
mysterious association with his resurrection (3, 10). [45] But
this wish and dynamic hope have their origin in the experience of « being captured by Christ Jesus » (*katelèmp-
thèn upo Christou Ièsou* ; 3, 12), « grasped by Christ
Jesus, » [46] which was precisely « the moment when Christ
seized hold of him on the Damascus road. » [47] Being seized
by Christ was an experience that turned his life upside
down, wholly transforming it. Suddenly, *because of* Christ
(*dia ton Christon* ; 3, 7), [48] what he was and what he
possessed, the privileges of his birth and education, his
religious and moral qualities, in short everything he had
hitherto valued (3, 7), was counted by him as « a loss »
(3, 7, 8). Consequently, he left everything through a radi-

---

45. See R. C. TANNEHILL's fine study, *Dying and Rising with
Christ : a Study of Pauline Theology*, Berlin, 1967 (especially 101-
104, 114-123) ; see also B. AHERN, « The Fellowship of His Suf-
ferings (Phil 3, 10), » in CBQ 22, 1960, 1-32 ; L. CERFAUX,
Le chrétien dans la théologie paulinienne, « Lectio divina » series 33,
Paris, 1962, 309-314 ; M. CARREZ, *De la souffrance à la gloire*,
Neuchâtel-Paris, 1964.
46. According to the translation suggested by M. GOGUEL,
Paulinisme et Johannisme, Paris, 1931, 48.
47. TOB, 594 note g (but see J.F. COLLANGE, *op. cit.*, 114).
48. On the meaning of *dia*, see P. BONNARD, *L'Epître de
Saint Paul...*, 63-64.

cal act of self-surrender. He eliminated it. [49] For ever.
Thenceforth he had but one desire : to accompany Christ ;
not like the apostles of the gospel narratives, on the roads
of Judea and Galilee, but on the path of his sufferings
and death (3, 10-11). The word *summorphizomenos* (3,
10), which we translate as « becoming like Christ in his
death » or « in growing conformity with his death, » literally signifies « taking the form of his death, » « walking with him *in his* death. » This path of Christ leads on
to the Resurrection, and Paul's hope is nurtured on the
desire to reach the end of that road by also attaining the
resurrection from the dead (3, 11). According to its lit-
eral meaning, the verb *katantaô*, to « reach, » is associated
with the idea of travelling (Ac *16*, 1 ; *18*, 19, 24 ; *20*, 15 ;
21, 7 ; *25*, 13 ; *27*, 12 ; *28*, 13, which all refer to Paul's
missionary travels). Paul sees his life as a journey with
Christ, a journey whose goal is the resurrection. [50] Without even looking for concordances, one cannot fail to note
the analogies with the apostles' vocation before the Passover event.

Certain of having been « seized by Jesus Christ, » constantly fascinated by the only One whose righteousness
counts, since human righteousness based on the Law is
empty (3, 9), Paul must nonetheless make a continuous
effort to advance, straining forward, forgetting what lies

---

49. « *Skubala* can be bluntly translated as dung, filth, mud, ex-
crements : what is untouchable and not even fit to look at once it
has been eliminated » (K. BARTH, *Commentary on Philippians*,
1927 ; see also F.W. BEARE, *op. cit.*, 116).
50. This is stressed by P. BONNARD, *op. cit.*, p. 67. In 3, 16
the verb *stoichein* (to walk firmly, without staggering) will be applied
to the Christian life as such (cf. Rm *4*, 12 ; Ga *5*, 25 ; *6*, 16).

behind (3, 12-14). He may never rest. Why ? Because despite the Damascus experience, he has not yet reached perfection (3, 12). « Seized by Christ, » he has not yet « seized the prize » (3, 12, 13). In all this his freedom is involved. But in answer to a grace. It is thus that his free- dom responds to « God's call to the life above, in Christ Jesus » (3, 14), the call which is conveyed by the inter- vention of Christ, inviting Paul to communion with him. In the race, Paul is not ahead of the other runners, but making his first acquaintance — albeit a demanding one — with a gift.

The text does not tell us by what means Paul intends to « seize » the prize of Christ and his Resurrection. [51] At all events, the verb *teletai*, « to become perfect » (3, 12), cannot be interpreted in a moral sense. Borrowed from the vocabulary of the mysteries, it is mainly expressive of the end of an initiation. Here it suggests the end of « Christ's path, » which is still unattainable in this life. [52] But from the other writings of Paul which refer to the Christian condition as such, we can glean a few valuable hints that enable us to understand the nature of the communion in Christ's Death of which the Letter to the Philippians speaks. [53]

If in conversion and baptism the believer dies to sin and receives the Spirit of Christ, he nonetheless remains influenced by what he has received from the old Adam.

---

51. On the precise object of this capturing, see *ibid.*, 67-68 (and TOB, 594 note g).

52. See F. W. BEARE, *op. cit.*, 129-130.

53. For a summary of these indications, see (in addition to the works cited above in footnote 45) James D.G. DUNN, *op. cit.*, 326-342.

Hence there is a tension, which is an inevitable source of suffering. In the believer the forces of life will be ceaselessly attacked by the forces of death, the Spirit will be assailed by the flesh. As long as he lives he will have to express the life of the Spirit through the heaviness and the onslaughts of his carnal being. Now it is precisely in this experience of weakness, of helplessness, that the true disciple — provided that he lives the experience in faith and hope — encounters Christ in his death and accompanies him on his journey. Then the power of the Lord rests upon him (2 Co *12,* 9-10 ; *13,* 4).

For there everything ties up and holds together. It is an experience of the power of God's grace, but in the poverty and weakness of the flesh (2 Co *4,* 7). Such an experience realistically embodies the tension between « I have been seized » and « I have not yet seized, » between the gratuitous *already* of Salvation and the *not yet* of the final resurrection. The believer's effort will lie in his refusal to escape this tension, his determination not to avoid it by simply surrendering to the old Adam or by clinging only to the powerful manifestations of the Spirit. For, as James Dunn tells us,

> Charismatic experience which tries to leave this paradox behind is potentially disastrous ; power without weakness is destructive ; only charismata which manifest power in weakness build up the community. This is clearly why Paul *never* boasts of his charismata, but rather of his weakness. [54]

Communion with Christ is therefore achieved through the experience of a new life constantly springing from the Cross. The Cross of the Lord Jesus, whose efficacy was

---

54. James D. G. DUNN, *op. cit.,* 329.

sown « once and for all » in the heart of mankind's destiny. But also the cross represented, *en Christo*, by the believer's struggle against the old Adam who lives on within him in a state of rebellion. And that is how it will be till the end of the road. Here all the dimensions of human existence are involved. In Paul's personal life, the apostolic ministry, for which he labours day and night, is one of the main places where this conflict between the flesh and the Spirit is being experienced (Ph 1, 21-26). [55] Here we are far from dry moralisms and grovelling pietisms ! As one of the greatest experts on Paul's thought writes :

> Paul's theology does not appear to be oriented towards an introspective examination of his own states of being. Rather it describes real states, using the philosophy of the time ; in short, what we would call the Christian being. One of the components of that Christian existence is our participation in the sufferings and death of Christ. Let us admit that this participation remains mysterious. It is indeed doubly mysterious : first, in that it affects our inmost being and transforms it by linking it with an event that really occurred in the life of Christ our Saviour ; and secondly, because God is not content to create merely a likeness within us, but goes further : he wishes this transformation to be more than just in the likeness of Christ and to continue within us the « reality » of life that was initially created in the dead and risen Christ. Thus the likeness approximates to identification. [56]

The specifically mystical dimension of the apostolic existence, the dimension that comes from the Lord's Spirit « seizing hold » of life at its very roots, develops more at

---

55. See L. CERFAUX, *op. cit.*, 311-313 ; and ID., « L'antinomie paulinienne de la vie apostolique, » in *Recueil Lucien Cerfaux*, T. 2, Gembloux, 1954, 455-467.
56. L. CERFAUX, *Le chrétien...*, 314.

this realistic depth than at the level of « marvels and wonders. » It is the demanding companionship with Christ on the paths of his Passion and his Cross, on the way to communion in his Resurrection, and not the jubilant experience of « spiritual » phenomena, that the Apostle seeks. For he knows that the Lord is calling him primarily to this goal.

For the religious who is « seized » by Christ in a mysterious moment that determines his life — and who may be immediately aware of the impact or only discover it gradually — the « following of Christ » is rooted in an experience analogous to that of Paul and the Apostles. A charismatic experience. Clearly, it is the experience of the labourer « overcome with joy » on suddenly discovering the treasure ; it is the experience of Paul caught in the conflict between flesh and Spirit, yet filled with the joy of Christ, a realistic joy growing and gaining strength beneath his sufferings.

At the root of every authentic religious life that is conscious of itself, one finds, as the primary and compelling motivation, not a *for...* but a *because of...* And here too the object of this *because of* is none other than Jesus Christ. One does not become a religious *for* something, *with a view* to something ; one enters the religious life *because of* Jesus Christ and his ascendency. The *for* will come later, necessarily, but in the radiance and as the evangelical fruit of the *because of.* In every vocation to follow Christ there is a moment of wonder before Christ, which fundamentally explains the postulant's choice of a particular Order, a particular form of evangelical service of mankind that perpetuates the vision of a founder or foundress. If the religious is not aware of this, he will never understand the *raison d'être* of the religious project, and having made a purely external act of profession, his life will drag on aimlessly.

That sense of wonder is undoubtedly bound up with an essential aspect of the act of faith : its contemplative aspect. To believe does not primarily mean to go forth, placing all one's living strength at the service of the Kingdom, consecrating it to the fight against human distress. Of course faith must entail *praxis* and cannot do otherwise; *praxis* is the sphere in which it unfolds and deepens.[57] For faith is a gift that shines in all its splendour only in the profound and courageous practice of the Gospel. The Christian penetrates the truth of Christ by acting in accordance with that truth. But before and beyond the practical action which it inspires and accomplishes, faith is the welcoming of the Lord. Moreover, it can be the motive force of action only because it revolves around the humble acceptance of a gift that comes from God. To believe is to receive, and not simply to discover. But this reception of God's gratuitous gift has the human fullness, which will condition the courageous action born of it, only if the heart welcomes his gift in a state of thanksgiving, praise and adoration. Otherwise the believer succumbs to an absolute voluntarism which denies human dignity. Man, the « image of God, » must be personally involved, with the whole of his being, in the most momentous action of his life : his « Yes » to God's invitation in Jesus Christ.

---

57. I have developed this point in J. M. R. TILLARD, A *Gospel Path : The Religious Life*, Brussels, Lumen Vitae Press, 1975, 49-73.

Now the contemplative gaze of faith — which, as I said earlier, is its prime and decisive aspect — strives mainly to reach that secret point where man stands alone before his God. This does not, of course, exclude the Christian conviction that faith's contemplative aspect is adequately acknowledged and celebrated only in the worshipping community. But there is a point where man, present to himself, becomes capable of truly hearing the word addressed not primarily to his group, to the assortment of beings surrounding him, but to him personally, challenging him as a particular individual. For if one truly wishes to understand the Gospel's message, it is impossible to deny that faith — which entrusts man with a heavy responsibility for the world — finds its pivot in a personal relationship, in a friendship. God is calling *this* man to enter with him into a relationship so meaningful that, in Jesus Christ, he will be *His* adopted son. The encounter, possibly initiated in a group experience or in the collective enthusiasm of a « charismatic » event, will be sealed as a profoundly genuine experience only in the silence, the joyful but secret silence, of the I-Thou relationship. And it is this moment of acknowledgment, of opening to the divine life, which is the contemplative moment I am attempting to describe. A moment so essential to faith that, without it, faith becomes meaningless. It is clear that in the religious life the endeavours of the « following of Christ » belong to this level of experience. They are the « Yes » to a word of Christ that aims to « seize hold » of the person in the depths of *his/her* desire.

The mainspring of the religious vocation, and of the many forms it takes, is therefore to be found at the contemplative level, that of man's attitude on discovering the fine pearl or the treasure. The person's gaze is then directed to Jesus Christ — inseparable from his Father and his Gospel — *because* He is what He is, and not *with a view to*... In other words, one contemplates Christ for his own sake : he and what is Mystery implies are an end in themselves. Such contemplation is a free, gratuitous act, an act of worship. In no sense utilitarian ; wholly devoid of petty moralism or cloying pietism. Here we are on another plane of existence.

That plane is doubtless the one that Jacques Maritain used to call « the sphere of the spirit at its source » and describe as the realm of poetic intuition, artistic genius, the mystical experience,[58] and above all as the dwelling of grace. He would speak of a « pre-consciousness » and a « spiritual supra-consciousness, » [59] hidden from the reasoning intelligence « in that density of the soul where all the soul's powers have their common origin. » [60] By this he meant that what is lived at this depth does not necessarily rise to the conscious level and may not be clearly grasped by the mind, although it inevitably influences the subject's life. Here we are beyond the frontiers of what people smugly call « normality, » forgetting that normality can only be what it is because it emerges from that creative

---

58. On the relationship between mysticism and poetry, see H. BREMOND : « poetic activity is a natural and profane adumbration of the mystical activity, » in *Prière et Poésie*, 208.

59. See Jacques and Raissa MARITAIN, *The Situation of Poetry*, New York, Philosophical Library, 1955, 45. 66 ; J. MARITAIN, *Creative Intuition in Art and Poetry*, New York, Bollingen Series, 1953 ; ID., *On the Grace and Humanity of Jesus*, London, Burns and Oates, 1967, 48-62. See also V. FRANKL, *The Unconscious God*, New York, Simon and Schuster, 1975, 60-70.

60. J. MARITAIN, *The Situation of Poetry*, 60.

and nourishing soil. Although in most cases it is appre-
hended intuitively and breaks through more clearly only
at privileged moments, what is lived at this depth of « spirit at its source » embraces the greatest gifts of man's
existence. Rather like fire smouldering beneath the ashes,
like « music in the soul of Mozart, » [61] or like the Damascus road experience in the soul of Paul.

The clear-minded religious is certain that, fundamentally, Christ's call resounds at that level ; not perhaps in
the early days when he enters the novitiate, but when,
like Simon Peter of the last chapter of John's Gospel, he
repeats — sometimes with tears and in suffering — the
« Yes » that one day determined the course of his life.
Enthusiasm ? Certainly. But one that is akin to the enthusiasm of the mystic, thirsting for his Lord even when he
is frightened by the dark night of doubt, or to the enthusiasm of the poet tormented by his *daimon.*

The Vow as the Gift of Self : Confession of Faith and Adoration

In the circumstances, the major decisions which essentially spring from that contemplative moment and
commit the believer's existence are in themselves an act
of worship. Moreover, the term « religious life, » used
since the turn of the fifth century to designate forms of
life dedicated to the « following of Christ, » is discreetly

---

61. J. MARITAIN, *On the Grace and Humanity of Jesus*, 65.

expressive of adoration. The apostles, fascinated by Jesus who was passing by and spoke to them in words that affected their inmost being, left everything *because of* him. Paul, « seized by Christ » on the Damascus road, left behind his privileges and his past *because of* him. In the same way, the religious comes to the confession of Jesus Christ as his sole *raison d'être* because of Christ whose call penetrates to the root of the great dynamic forces which fashion him and by which he builds his world.

It cannot be too strongly emphasized that it is only in this perspective that the vow is meaningful. Anyone who fails to grasp this point is in danger of surrendering to a life of sheer masochism. The vows must be conceived as a confession of faith expressed not in words but by the heart, the flesh and the spirit. They are a prostration of the whole being — captured in those deep roots which are the sexual drive, the desire to possess and the thirst for power — before the One whom Christians acknowledge as the Lord of their existence. A prostration made not by the religion of external rites, jubilation and « marvels, » but by that religion of which the prophets spoke and which is life itself led as a homage to God. Long before they imply renunciation, mortification, asceticism, dyng to oneself, sacrifice and the subjugation of the will, the vows are adoration. Long before being « a means of freeing a person for the service of the Church, » they are a God-centred act. Long before expressing the generosity of the believer, determined to sweat blood in order to build up the Kingdom, they are a hymn to the Lord of that Kingdom. That is precisely why they are renunciation, a means of making the person more free, and the generous act of

the believer. In other words, the « following of Christ, »
which casts man into the most demanding and concrete
diakonia of the Kingdom, is primarily doxological.] When
the ancient texts stated that one became Brother X, Sister
Y or Father Z « for the glory of God, » they were much
nearer to the truth than some commentators would have
us believe.

This all-embracing, doxological quality gives action its
true greatness. For it is in these circumstances that the
apostolic commitment, lived in the very name of the decision to « leave everything » *because of* Christ, is akin to
adoration. For it is part of the whole process whereby man
subjects his powerful instincts and drives to the sovereignty of Christ Jesus. Action is not externally added to
his effort to find self-fulfilment in his surge of desire,
but merely actualizes that surging desire. Just as in the
case of Paul and the apostles the fact of accompanying
Jesus on the paths of his ministry or of preaching the
Gospel throughout the empire is implicit in the « leave
everything *because of* him, » and can be understood only
in the light of what first awakened that attachment, the
work of the religious « for the Gospel » is intimately bound
up with the decision he has taken in regard to the enjoy-
ment of the senses, ownership and power. His work for the
Gospel does not depend on another decision that is added
to and strengthens the initial one. It is the same ascendency
of Christ which, alone, accounts for his one, indivisible
decision : to leave everything and to give all his future
action a goal that is logically consistent with the absolute
attraction exercised by the One he wishes to follow. From
the outset his activity, or at least its line of force, will not
be directed towards the mere quenching of « desire »

considered in terms of its three roots (sexuality, the need
to possess, the thirst for power) so that, having overcome
that desire, he may further his legitimate ambitions, but
will be an endeavour to place the whole of himself, including his natural drives and ambitions, at the service
of the Kingdom.

This is a very important point. There can be no question
of « switching off » one's sexuality by denying one's
specific nature as a man or a woman (in any case, this
is hardly possible), or of refusing to develop one's talents
because of their latent power, or of stripping oneself of so
many possessions that one becomes a social parasite. The
religious must know how to integrate sexuality, ownership
and power with his state of life in such a way that those
very drives which fashion him as a human being serve
the absolute conviction that governs his life : the Lord
Jesus alone — seen in his relation to the Father and to
the Kingdom — is wholly fascinating ; he alone is pre-
ferable to everything else. The vows of poverty, chastity
and obedience, correctly understood, are geared to action.
From this standpoint, one cannot accept the simplistic
but so widespread assertion — found even in some Consti-
tutions — that the religious project concerns being, not
action. What a shallow philosophy and myopic view of
reality that is ! In the life of the religious it is quite impossible to make a clear-cut distinction between being
and action, and this applies as much to apostolic action
as to the type of activity which, for monks and contemplatives of every order, is the humble daily task whose
kernel is the liturgical celebration of God's glory. It is
thus that life finds its unity from the very first moment,
the contemplative moment. A charismatic moment, if ever

there was one, for it is then that the Spirit's gift trans-
forms existence itself.

Moreover, in taking these « three vows, » the religious
is consecrating the whole of himself — and now we
understand why this is so. [62] In a previous study I have
explained how, at a rather late date, [63] this triad, which
was to become so important in the West, was initially
understood as a « symbol » (*sacramentum*) of the gift
of the whole person. In the thought of the early centuries,
still faithfully echoed by Thomas Aquinas, the monk or
the religious did not simply make God an offering of
his basic drives : sexuality, ownership and power. He
offered them to God because he wished to offer the
whole of himself. For, in their dynamic power, those
drives mark out the sphere of human desire and self-fulfilment. And it is clear that, regardlesss of its nature, action
is always dependent on them. There is a classical image
which expresses this very eloquently, although it refers
not to man's basic drives but to the forms in which the
religious project invests them : poverty, chastity and obedience are the three main roots by which the tree strikes
deep into the evangelical soil and draws its nourishment.
The tiniest hairs at the end of the rootlets are dependent on
this triple tap root. But the main roots and the rootlets
exist for the tree, and it is the tree that counts. The habit
of isolating the classical triad and failing to link it up
with the total human reality which the religious project
embraces has engendered the formalisms that we deplore

---

62. See J. M. R. TILLARD, *Devant Dieu et pour le monde : le
projet des religieux,* « Cogitatio fidei » series 75, Paris, 1974, 353-397.
63. *Ibid.,* 119-123, 387-397.

today. Many religious lives are like tree-stumps, still rooted in the soil, but deprived of life because they have no trunk, no branches or leaves or fruit, and these are the splendour of the tree.

Contemplative Attention and the « Following of Christ »

This brings us to a first conclusion. For a religious, no matter whether he belongs to a contemplative order or to a more active congregation, there can be no true « life in the Spirit » unless he continues to honour and to observe that pause for the contemplative moment, the moment when Christ's call found an echo in him.

I should not like this statement to be interpreted as a kind of secret attempt to remonasticize the religious life. This would be a complete misunderstanding of my thought. I am speaking of a wholly different level of existence : not the level of rites, of forms of prayer, of styles distinguishing this form of life from that one, or more or less separating both from the ordinary existence of men in our modern societies. No. What I have in mind is the profound aim of life, the gaze of the heart, that mysterious presence of Christ in the thick of action — the presence to which a Madeleine Delbrêl in our time or a Lancelot Andrewes in seventeenth century Anglicanism are witnesses. Besides (and this is an astonishing discovery), the most compelling testimonies come not from monks buried in the peace of the cloisters, but from a Dominic trudging along the highways (« *aut de Deo, aut cum Deo* »), an Ignatius Loyola breaking away from the monastic tradition, a Vincent of Paul forbidding his « daughters » to be an enclosed order, a Catherine of Siena flitting « like a bee » from one task to another, and an Adelaïde de Cicé helping Père de Clorivière to institute, in the turmoil of the French Revolution, a new type of religious life led in the heart of the world.

There is nothing monastic about these examples. But, at the same time, let us not be naive or foolishly idealistic. The gaze of the heart soon loses its limpidity if the person does not nourish himself on prayer — the style of prayer matters little — and does not immerse himself in silence from time to time. Some assertions about « discovering God in action itself, » which are intuitively correct (for by loving and serving mankind as the Gospel urges, we are « communicating » in the ways of God) need to be completed and carefully qualified. But what I wish to stress is the absolute, vital necessity of keeping as the backcloth of life and action the attentiveness to God and the realistic, mature, in no sense juvenile enthusiasm for Jesus Christ which coincided with the Lord's call. Although it is right to say that a vocation is not wasted — for it comes from God — we must nonetheless add that man can gradually fill his heart with so much noise and so many centres of interest that the word which sent him out to serve no longer resounds in it.

Let us note the difference between the wholly spiritual interiority of that contemplative, adoring and doxological attentiveness and the exteriority of some of the charismatic manifestations mentioned by Paul. The latter are directly subordinated to a *for...* and they are not anchored in the

Christian by the necessary pause to contemplate their source. Moved by the Spirit, this man prophesies while another « speaks in tongues. » Such gifts are meaningful only in so far as they benefit the community, and Paul goes so far as to make their usefulness to the whole assembly a criterion for discerning their authenticity : « Since you aspire to spiritual gifts, concentrate on those, strive to excel in those that build up the church » (1 Co 14, 12) ; « In the community I would rather say five meaningful words in order to instruct others than ten thousand words in a tongue » (14, 19) ; « If there is no interpreter present, they must keep quiet in church and speak only to themselves and to God » (14, 28). Here we are dealing with charismatic *phenomena* rather than with the *experience of* the Spirit, if we give the word « experience » the meaning it has always had in the great Christian Tradition.

But elsewhere Paul does use the word charism in a way that instantly evokes a pause to contemplate the inner experience. In particular, he does so in 1 Corinthians 7. There the fact of being *agamos* (unmarried) is indicated as a charism (1 Co 7, 7). The context shows that what makes this gift of the Spirit meaningful is not primarily its usefulness to the community but the believer's personal relationship with his Lord (see also 7, 32-34). [64] It is, in fact, a charism that, from the earliest times and universally, the « following of Christ » incorporated into the religious life. Faithful to Paul's intuitions, the « following

---

64. See G. HASENHUETTL, *op. cit.*, 153-157 ; James D. G. DUNN, *op. cit.*, 206 ; F. GRAU, *Der Neutestamentliche Begriff charisma*, Tübingen, 1946, 64-69.

of Christ » was to maintain that, like all its other con-
stituent elements, the unmarried state makes sense only
if the follower manifests an « unconditional dependence
on and openness to God.» [65] Bearing in mind the particular
vocation of each religious family, however, it was to link
the unmarried state with the evangelical service which it
postulates. In other words, it was to incorporate that state
within the broader charism which defines it : the charism
of an existence intent on serving the Kingdom, but because
fundamentally it is engrossed in God.

*

*   *

At this point of our reflection, can we not affirm that,
although it does strive for and promote effective action
that serves the Kingdom, the « following of Christ » —
even in the most active « apostolic » congregations —
witnesses mainly to the Gospel's mystical and charismatic
dimension ? In the line of Paul's experience, it proclaims
that since the Cross of Golgotha, the believer's impact
is no longer to be sought primarily in its effectiveness but
in its proximity to the Lord and his Spirit. Nothing is
more necessary than the apostle's toil and sweat, but what
would they be worth without his efforts to imprint
on them the traits of Christ in his Passover ? Commenting
on Luther's principle that « man is justified by faith, »
J. Moltmann writes :

> No form of action leads us from an inhuman to a human
> reality of man, for there is no way to get from doing to being.

---

65. James D. G. DUNN, *op cit.*, 256.

> What man is in his ground precedes what he does and mani-
> fests itself in his actions. [66]

According to the logic of the Gospel, the only hand that
can actively distribute is the one that is, first of all, ready
to open in receiving. If it is true that the essential
characteristic of charism is that it is not the product of
man's ability or sanctity but the seal of the Spirit, [67] it
is not surprising that the « following of Christ » witnesses
to this priority of receivng over generosity. This is due
to its charismatic nature.

---

66. Jürgen MOLTMANN, *Theology and Joy*, London, SCM Press,
1973, 66.
67. Well emphasized by James D. G. DUNN, *op. cit.*, 254-256.

II

The Search for God

The gaze that contemplates God because the person has
been « seized by Christ » belongs, as we noted earlier, to
a depth of the human mind that transcends the habitual
level of the reasoning intelligence. The quality of the religious life, considered more in terms of a God-centred faith
than of moral perfection, depends upon it. That is why it
is a lasting gaze, sorrowful perhaps but always true, even
when the religious is aware of his sinfulness, his wretched-
ness and the stigma of evil in his flesh. Like the gaze of
David — « God's anointed one » — after he had sinned.
Like the gaze of Peter. It should not, therefore, be confused with the « search for God, » which the religious
project also demands, but which belongs to a wholly different level of experience : that of the moral life and the
quest for perfection. A perfection, let us already note,
which leads into contemplation.

Although the « search for God » is carried out by the
grace of the Spirit (how could it be otherwise ?), and

although Paul reminds us that its sanctuary is communion in the Cross of Christ, it is obvious that it mainly involves human effort and the seeker's generous fidelity to the grace he has received. It designates man's response envisaged, this time, not under its aspect of wonder at the sight of the pearl or the treasure, but from the standpoint of its ethical requirement. For the search for God is expressive of all the energy, the virtue and the love that must be invested in the quest by the man who — having been « seized by Christ » — hopes to enter one day into His glory. Dietrich Bonhoeffer, commenting on the Sermon on the Mount in his book *The Cost of Discipleship*, speaks of « costly grace. » [1] Indeed, Christian grace finds a perfect balance in this dialectical tension between God's initiative and man's response. Encountered by God, gratuitously, in Jesus Christ, the Christian has to enter into the gift of this encounter, day after day, with his living strength, in order to « see God face to face » at the end of the road, and only at the end : « for now we see in a mirror dimly, but then face to face. Now I know in part ; but then I shall know as fully as I am known » (1 Co 13, 12).

The « search for God » theme has a long biblical history. [2] Although the expression sometimes means speaking

1. D. BONHOEFFER, *The Cost of Discipleship*, London, SCM Press, 1948, 37-39.
2. On this theme see especially G. TURBESSI, « Quaerere Deum ; il tema della ' ricerca di Dio ' nella S. Scrittura, » in *Rivista Biblica* 10, 1962, 282-296 ; ID., « Quaerere Deum. Il tema della ' ricerca di Dio ' nell'ambiente ellenistico e giudaico contemporaneo al N.T., » in *Studiorum Paulinorum Congressus Internationalis Catholicus 1961,* T. 2 (*Analecta Biblica* 18), Rome, 1963, 383-398 ; ID., « ' Quaerere

to God in order to consult him or to find support in him alone and not in other gods, and although the Wisdom Books lend that search a markedly intellectual colour, [8] it generally signifies in the Old Testament observing the clauses of the Covenant by faithfully endeavouring to obey God's wishes (cf. Is *51*, 1 ; *55*, 6 ; *58*, 2 ; Jr *10*, 21 ; *50*, 4-5 ; Am *5*, 4, 6, 14 ; Ps *14*, 1-3 ; *119*, 1-3, 10 ; etc.).

In this sense, the Qumran Community Rule states that the members have come together

> that they may seek God..., and do what is good and right before Him as 'He commanded by the hand of Moses and all His servants the Prophets ; that they may love all that He has chosen and hate all that He has rejected ; that they may abstain from all evil and hold fast to all good ; that they may practise truth, righteousness, and justice upon earth and no longer stubbornly follow a sinful heart and lustful eyes committing all manner of evil. He shall admit into the Covenant of Grace all those who have freely devoted themselves to the observance of God's precepts, that they may be joined to the counsel of God and may live perfectly before Him in accordance with all that has been revealed concerning their appointed times, and that they may love all the sons of light, each according to his lot in God's design, and hate all the sons of darkness, each according to his guilt in God's vengeance. [4]

Deum ' ; la ' ricerca di Dio ' in antichi testi cristiani, » in *Rivista di Ascetica e Mistica* 9, 1964, 241-255 ; ID., « ' Quaerere Deum ' ; il tema della ' ricerca di Dio ' nella gnosi e nello gnosticismo, » in *Benedictina* 18, 1971, 1-31 ; S. LEGASSE, *L'appel du riche, contribution à l'étude des fondements scripturaires de l'état religieux*, Paris, 1966, 175-183 ; J. DUPONT, *Les Béatitudes*, T. 3, Paris, 1973, 272-305.

3. J. DUPONT, *loc. cit.*, 299-300 ; S. LEGASSE, *op. cit.*, 177 ; G. TURBESSI, « Quaerere ... nella S. Scrittura, » 291-293.

4. *The Community Rule*, I : 1-10 ; trans. G. VERMES, *The Dead Sea Scrolls in English*, London, Penguin, 1975 (2nd ed.), 72.

« To seek God » basically means to seek righteousness
by endeavouring to obey the Law. In the Sermon on the
Mount, Matthew, attentive to the demands of the new
Law and what they imply : the faithful doing of God's
will, stresses this point : « Seek first his Kingdom and his
righteousness, and all these other things will be given to
you as well » (6, 33). To enter the Kingdom, it is not
enough to say « Lord, Lord » ; one has to do the will of
the heavenly Father (7, 21). [5]

When in the conversation between Jesus and the rich
young man, Matthew (the only evangelist to do so) intro-
duces the idea of « perfection, » it is to this basic requirement, righteousness, that he refers. [6] The exemplary Jew,
who since childhood has « kept » all the commandments
of the old Law (Mt 19, 17-20) — the path towards « eternal life » (19, 16) and « entry into the Kingdom » (19,
23-24) — is asked by Jesus to take a further step which
will introduce him into the new righteousness, the one
that comes from practising the Torah as renewed by
Him. [7] Now, this means, in fact, surrendering his life to
Jesus, « offering it unreservedly to his ' yoke ' and his
' burden '. » [8] In this light the « follow me » becomes re-
markably meaningful :

> « Following Jesus » is the act of the man who places his
> life at the Saviour's disposal by joining the community which
> unites him to His person. Such an act is the very opposite

---

5. J. DUPONT, *op. cit.*, 305. On the synonymity between « to
seek righteousness » and « to seek YHWH » in the language of the
Bible, see S. LEGASSE, *op. cit.*, 177.
6. S. LEGASSE, *op. cit.*, shows this clearly.
7. See S. LEGASSE, *ibid.*, 194, 196.
8. S. LEGASSE, *ibid.*, 117.

of purely external or verbal adherence, for it engages his moral life : to be Jesus' disciple is not simply to proclaim his sovereignty, but also to belong to the society of those who wish to do the heavenly Father's messianic will (Mt 7, 21) of which Jesus is the interpreter, and who wish to listen to his words and put them into practice (7, 24). For Matthew, it means living the Torah interpreted by Christ, seeking the Kingdom and God's righteousness, and consequently refusing to be obsessed by the things of this world, especially wealth, even at the price of the most costly sacrifices. It also means accepting suffering, separation and persecution for the love of Jesus (16, 24-26) and by sharing what he has himself been willing to undergo (10, 24-25). It is only thus that one « follows » Jesus and can rightly call oneself his disciple, and hope to be ultimately rewarded by him (16, 27). [9]

This aspect of the « following of Christ » is « at once second and moral. » For

it is no longer a question of the initial act which tears the disciple away from his family and his possessions in order to introduce him into the intimate circle of friends who follow Jesus on his evangelizing journeys. We are dealing here with the moral effort of a whole life, already given to the Lord through baptism, but which must be always consistent with the logic of its original commitment. [10]

The definition of the *sequela Christi* or of the religious life as a « search for perfection » belongs to this second, moral level ; so too does the content of the great religious Rules. The sense of wonder before Christ and the God-centred gratuitousness of the vows are incarnated in obedience to the law of the Kingdom. A conscious and radical obedience. The biblical context tells us much about this « secondary level. » It is important to see how it does this.

---

9. *Ibid.*, 207-208.
10. *Ibid.*, 208, note 78.

But we are thus entering a domain where everything has
subtle shades of meaning and has to be carefully qualified.

The Monastic Aim

I have just mentioned the *Community Rule,* discovered
in 1947 with other important texts in the caves of Khirbet
Qumran near the shores of the Dead Sea. [11] We must

---

11. The *Community Rule* is translated and commented on in
J. CARMIGNAC and P. GUILBERT, *les textes de Qumran traduits
et annotés - T. 1 : La Règle de la communauté. La Règle de la
guerre. Les Hymnes,* Paris, 1961, 9-80 ; A. DUPONT-SOMMER,
The Essene Writings from Qumran, Oxford, Basil Black, 1961,
68-113 ; M. BURROWS, *The Dead Sea Scrolls,* New York, 1956 ;
William Hugh BROWNLEE, *The Dead Sea Manual of Discipline,
translation and notes,* series : *Bulletin of the American Schools of
Oriental Research. Supplementary Studies* Nos. 10-12, New Haven,
1951 (an excellent translation) ; G. VERMES, *The Dead Sea Scrolls
in English,* London, Penguin, 1975, 2nd ed. (with a good Introduction, pp. 11-15, and a selected bibliography) ; P. WERNBERG-
MOELLER, *The Manual of Discipline, translated and annotated
with an Introduction,* series : *Studies on the Texts of the Desert
of Judah,* vol. 1, Leiden, 1957 ; A. VINCENT, *Les Manuscrits
hébreux du Désert de Juda,* Paris, 1955, 120-147 ; J. VAN DER
PLOEG, *Le Manuel de Discipline des Rouleaux de la Mer Morte,* in
Bibliotheca Orientalis, 1951, 113-125.
The *Congregation Rule,* appended to *The Community Rule,* has
been edited and translated by D. BARTHELEMY, *Qumran Cave 1,*
109-111, series : *Discoveries in the Judean Desert,* vol. 1, Oxford,
1955. See also A. DUPONT-SOMMER, *op. cit.,* 119-123.
As enlightening studies on the point that concerns us here, see,
in addition to A. DUPONT-SOMMER's introductions : D. HOW-
LETT, *Les Esséniens et le christianisme,* Paris, 1958 ; P. BENOIT,
review of Chaim RABIN, *Qumran Studies,* series : *Studia Judaica II,*

dwell for a while on this document, for it opens up a wide horizon. The Manual of Discipline which records this Rule is, despite notable divergences, closely related to the *Damascus Rule,* already published in 1910 following the discovery in Cairo of two incomplete medieval copies. Extensive fragments of the same document have been recovered from the Qumran caves. [12] What can a theology which carefully confines itself to its own field learn from all this ? A great deal.

The Community Rule spontaneously evokes a monastic life style, [13] that of a group of ardent believers whose spirit is that of a Jewish sect but whose structure resembles that

Oxford, 1957, in *Revue Biblique* 1959, 118-121 ; P. GUILBERT, « Le plan de la Règle de la communauté, » in *Revue de Qumrân* 1, 1959, 323-344 ; J. T. MILIK, review of P. WERNBERG-MOELLER, *The Manual of Discipline,* in *Revue Biblique* 1960, 410-416 (giving the variants of the different manuscripts of the Rule) ; in collaboration, *Recherches Bibliques IV. La Secte de Qumrân et les Origines du Christianisme,* Paris, 1959 ; for the whole context, see M. SIMON, *Les sectes juives au temps de Jésus,* Paris, 1960.

12. For *The Damascus Document,* see S. SCHECHTER, *Documents of Jewish Sectaries,* vol. 1, *Fragments of a Zadokite Work, Provided with an English Translation, Introduction and Notes,* Cambridge, 1910 ; Chaim RABIN, *The Zadokite Documents,* Oxford, 1954 ; Solomon ZEITLIN, *The Zadokite Fragments, Facsimile of the Manuscripts in the Cairo Genizah Collection in the Possession of the University Library, Cambridge, England,* Philadelphia, 1952 (radical position) ; the text can be found more easily in R. H. CHARLES, *Apocrypha and Pseudoepigrapha of the Old Testament,* T. 2, Oxford, 1920, 785-834.

13. E.F. SUTCLIFFE, *The Monks of Qumran,* London, 1960, gives this title to his study and translation of the texts. See also F. NUTSCHER, « Jüdische Mönchgemeinde und Ursprung des Christentums nach dem Jüngst am Toten Meer aufgefundenen hebräischen Handschriften, » in *Bibel und Kirche* 1952, 21-38.

of a religious order with its organization, [14] its hierarchy, [15] its common life, [16] its progressive initiation rites (including

---

14. Thus, where assemblies are concerned, « the Priests shall sit first, and the elders second, and all the rest of the people according to their rank. And thus shall they be questioned concerning the Law, and concerning any counsel or matter coming before the Congregation, each man bringing his knowledge to the Council of the Community. No man shall interrupt a companion before his speech has ended, nor speak before a man of higher rank ; each man shall speak in his turn. And in an Assembly of the Congregation no man shall speak without the consent of the Congregation, nor indeed of the Guardian of the Congregation. Should any man wish to speak to the Congregation, yet not be in a position to question the Council of the Community, let him rise to his feet and say : ' I have something to say to the Congregation. ' If they command him to speak, he shall speak » (VI : 8-13 ; trans. G. VERMES, 81 ; cf. *ibid.*, 25-26). On the supreme Council, see VIII : 1-4, G. VERMES, 85, 86.

15. « The Priests shall enter first, ranked one after another according to the perfection of their spirit ; then the Levites ; and thirdly, all the people one after another... that every Israelite may know his place in the Community of God according to the everlasting design. No man shall move down from his place nor move up from his allotted position » (II : 19-24 ; G. VERMES, 74 ; see VI : 2-12, G. VERMES, 80-81).

16. « The man of lesser rank shall obey the greater in matters of work and money. They shall eat in common and pray in common and deliberate in common. Wherever there are ten men of the Council of the Community there shall not lack a Priest among them. And they shall all sit before him according to their rank and shall be asked their counsel in all things in that order. And when the table has been prepared for eating, and the new wine for drinking, the Priest shall be the first to stretch out his hand to bless the first-fruits of the bread and new wine. And where the ten are, there shall never lack a man among them who shall study the Law continually, day and night, concerning the right conduct of a man with his companion. And the Congregation shall watch in community for a third of every night of the year, to read the Book and to study the Law and to pray together » (VI : 2-8 ; G. VERMES, 80-81). See A. DUPONT-SOMMER, *The Essene Writings ...*, 85.

the novitiate), [17] its binding oath, [18] its emphasis on the meditation of Scripture and prayer, [19] and its penal code. [20]

---

17. « Every man, born of Israel, who freely pledges himself to join the Council of the Community, shall be examined by the Guardian at the head of the Congregation concerning his understanding and his deeds. If he is fitted to the discipline, he shall admit him into the Covenant that he may be converted to the truth and depart from all falsehood ; and he shall instruct him in all the rules of the Community. And later, when he comes to stand before the Congregation, they shall all deliberate his case, and according to the decisions of the Council of the Congregation, he shall either enter or depart. After he has entered the Council of the Community, he shall not touch the pure Meal of the Congregation until one full year is completed, and until he has been examined concerning his spirit and deeds ; nor shall he have any share of the property of the Congregation. Then when he has completed one year within the Community, the Congregation shall deliberate his case with regard to his understanding and observance of the Law. And if it be his destiny, according to the judgement of the Priests and the multitude of the men of the Covenant, to enter the company of the Community, his property and earnings shall be handed over to the Bursar of the Congregation who shall register it to his account and shall not spend it for the Congregation. He shall not touch the Drink of the Congregation until he has completed a second year among the men of the Community. But when the second year has passed, he shall be examined, and if it be his destiny, according to the judgement of the Congregation, to enter the Community, then he shall be inscribed among his brethren in the order of his rank for the Law, and for justice, and for the pure Meal ; his property shall be merged and he shall offer his counsel and judgement to the Community » (VI : 13-23 ; G. VERMES, 81-82).

18. « Whoever approaches the Council of the Community shall enter the Covenant of God in the presence of all who have freely pledged themselves. He shall undertake by a binding oath to return with all his heart and soul to every commandment of the Law of Moses in accordance with all that has been revealed of it to the sons of Zadok, the Keepers of the Covenant and Seekers of His will, and to the multitude of the men of the Covenant who together have

(See notes 19 and 20, next page).

Moreover, the archaeological excavation of the site itself, which was already known but as yet not methodically explored, has brought to light the ruins of a settlement which undoubtedly suggests a « monastery » with its kitchen, its scriptorium where manuscripts were copied, workshops, several community halls and a large meeting-hall, water cisterns for ritual baths, and a cemetery. [21] Various clues (such as coins and signs of a violent destruction of the buildings) show that the settlement was inhabited from about the 2nd century B.C. to A.D. 68. Clearly, there is a direct link between this « monastic » architecture and the « monastic » Rule of which a complete manuscript has been discovered in the caves of Khirbet Qumran along with fragments of ten other manuscripts. In the region where the Baptist recruited his disciples (notably those who were to « follow Jesus »), near the place where Jesus himself retired at the beginning of his ministry, Jewish believers were leading a common life that endeavoured to be wholly faithful to the Covenant and had « monastic » features.

---

freely pledged themselves to His truth and to walking in the way of His delight. And he shall undertake by the Covenant to separate from all the men of falsehood who walk in the way of wickedness. For all are not reckoned in His Covenant. They have neither inquired nor sought after Him concerning His laws ... » (V : 7-12 ; G. VERMES, 79). See A. DUPONT-SOMMER, *The Essene Writings...*, 83.

19. See especially, X : 1-17, G. VERMES, 88-92 ; I, 18-20, G. VERMES, 72-73.

20. See VI : 24 - VII : 25, G. VERMES, 82-84.

21. On this entire question see J.T. MILIK, *Dix ans de découvertes dans le Désert de Juda*, Paris, 1957 ; see also Yigael YADIN, *The Message of the Scrolls*, New York, 1957, 60-72 and A. DUPONT-SOMMER, *The Essene Writings ...*, 62-67.

Now, the ideal that inspires such a life is none other than the « search for God, » in accordance with His commandments to Moses and the prophets [22] and with « all that has been revealed (of them) to the sons of Zadok, the Keepers of the Covenant and *Seekers* of His will. » [23] Together, then, they « sought after » and studied his precepts [24] and practised all the virtues. [25] The aim of this austere and disciplined existence in the wilderness was to study the Law, to understand and practise it, in order to « convert one's life » [26] and thus to be united with God.

Here, as in the biblical Books of Wisdom and in the writings of Philo Judaeus, a more intellectual preoccupation, inseparable from the ethical « search » for God, is evidenced : the desire to « contemplate » the Divinity with the human mind. This must be achieved by meditating the Law and the Prophets. As we know, Philo (c. 20 B.C. — 50 A.D.) extols this contemplation to which man aspires. [27] But neither Philo nor our Qumran ascetics attempt to

---

22. See I : 1-3, G. VERMES, 72.
23. See V : 9, G. VERMES, 79.
24. See V : 11. G. VERMES, 79.
25. See especially V : 1-7, G. VERMES, 78-79.
26. Conversion is a central theme. See III : 1-12, G. VERMES, 74-76.
27. On Philo's thought in this domain, see G. TURBESSI, « Quaerere... contemporaneo al N. T., » 391-395 (a brief but excellent synthesis); see also E. BREHIER, *Les idées philosophiques et religieuses de Philon d'Alexandrie*, Paris, 1925, 206-249 ; E.R. GOODENOUGH, *Introduction to Philo Judaeus*, New Haven, 1940 (a very absolute position); E. VANDERLINDEN, « Les divers modes de connaissance de Dieu selon Philon d'Alexandrie, » in *Mél. Sc. Rel.* 4, 1947, 285-304 ; J. DUPONT, *Gnosis*, Louvain-Paris, 1949, 361-367 ; A.J. FESTUGIERE, *La Révélation d'Hermès Trismegiste*, T. 2 - *Le Dieu cosmique*, Paris, 1949, 519-572 ; J. DANIELOU, *Philon d'Alexandrie*,

separate this more intellectual quest from the ethical and
cultic context in which it is pursued and acquires its seal
of authenticity. [28] For them, the intellect, the will and the
heart are inseparably united. The aim is the union of the
whole person with God. Moreover, the writings of the sect
are penetrated with the firmly underlined conviction that
human efforts can be successful only if they are « objects
of God's love and fidelity. » [29] For they proclaim that
man's heart is poor and unworthy of God's benevolence :
hence « humility and trust are the virtues which characterize the relationships of the members of the Community
with God. » [30] The Rule ends with two pages of such
beauty that we must pause to admire the following extracts :

> As for me, my justification is with God. In His hand are
> the perfection of my way and ,the uprightness of my heart. He
> will wipe out my transgression through His righteousness. For
> my light has sprung from the source of His knowledge ; my
> eyes have beheld His marvellous deeds, and the light of my
> heart, the mystery to come. He that is everlasting is the
> support of my right hand...
> As for me, if I stumble, the mercies of God shall be my
> eternal salvation. If I stagger because of the sin of flesh,
> my justification shall be by the righteousness of God which
> endures for ever. When my distress is unleashed, He will
> deliver my soul from ,the pit and will direct my steps to the
> way. He will draw me near by His grace, and by His mercy

Paris, 1958, 183-198 (and 143-149) ; F. DUMAS, Introduction to
PHILO's *De vita contemplativa,* series : *Les Œuvres de Philon
d'Alexandrie 29,* Paris, 1963.

28. This is well brought out by G. TURBESSI, « Quaerere ... contemporaneo al N. T., » 396, 398. See also ID., « Quaerere Deum ...
antichi testi cristiani, » 241-242.

29. See the beautiful texts cited by G. VERMES, *op. cit.,* 39-41.

30. G. VERMES, *ibid.,* 41.

will He bring my justification. He will judge me in the righteousness of His truth and in the greatness of His goodness He will pardon all my sins. Through His righteousness He will cleanse me of the uncleanness of man and of the sins of the children of men, that I may confess to God His righteousness, and His majesty to the Most High.

Blessed art Thou, my God, who openest the heart of Thy servant to knowledge ! Establish all his deeds in righteousness..., grant that the son of Thy handmaid may stand before Thee for ever. For without Thee no way is perfect, and without Thy will nothing is done. It is Thou who has taught all knowledge and all things come to pass by Thy will. There is none beside Thee to dispute Thy counsel or to understand all Thy holy design, or to contemplate the depth of Thy mysteries and the power of Thy might. Who can endure Thy glory, and what is the son of man in the midst of Thy wonderful deeds ? What shall one born of woman be accounted before Thee ? ... He is but a shape, but moulded clay, and inclines towards dust. What shall hand-moulded clay reply ? What counsel shall it understand ? [31]

Our pause to admire these extracts is by no means a digression. It leads to the heart of the monastic and « religious » problem. As I said earlier, the sense of wonder in which the project of the « following of Christ » is rooted, and which is the basic, original moment of that vocation, urges man to go deeper and deeper into the living encounter with God, and hence to enter into the ethical demands of the search for God. The Qumran community is an explicit example of the form given to this quest, within the People of God, before Christ, by brethren endeavouring to seek God together.

Following the experts on the Qumran texts, I have even slipped in the word « monachism. » This is important. For Qumran is not the only instance of such group-

31. XI : 1-22, G. VERMES, 37-42.

ings which, as we now know, existed on the fringe of
pre-Christian Jewish society. Thanks to Pliny the Elder,
the historian Josephus and Philo, [32] we already knew, long
before the discovery of the Dead Sea scrolls, of the existence in Judaism of a sect living apart from the populace
and called the Essenes. These men sought God together
by meditating the Law and practising rigorous asceticism,
poverty and celibacy. Pliny tells us of a group dwelling on
the Western shore of the Dead Sea, but Josephus specifies
that a colony was to be found in several towns. [33] And
this appears to be confirmed by Philo. [34] Although some
scholars still hesitate to commit themselves, it is generally
agreed that the Qumran « monastery » was one of these
colonies, and more precisely the one described by Pliny. [35]

---

32. PLINY, *Hist. nat.*, V : 17, 4 ; Flavius JOSEPHUS, *Bell.*, II :
8, 2-13 ; ID., *Ant.* XVIII : 1-5 ; PHILO, *Quod omnis probus liber
sit*, 75-91 ; ID., *Apology of the Jews* (in EUSEBIUS OF CAESAREA,
Praeparatio evangelica VIII, 11). These texts are translated in A.
DUPONT-SOMMER, *The Essene Writings...* 21-38.

33. « They do not dwell in just one town, but in each town
several of them form a colony » (*Bell* : II : 8, 4).

34. See M. PETIT, *Quod omnis probus liber sit. Introduction, texte,
traduction et notes*, series : *Les œuvres de Philon d'Alexandrie* 28,
Paris, 1974, 198 (and note 1).

35. « The Essenic thesis has won... an ever-increasing number of
supporters. Today it is readily accepted by the vast majority of critics » ;
« If in this region (Pliny) knows of only one grouping of hermits, whom
he calls the Essenes, and since the Qumran settlement corresponds
exactly to the type of life briefly described by Pliny, and set out in
greater detail by Philo and particularly by Josephus, we are certainly
entitled to recognize in this site an Essenic establishment, and probably
the ' mother house ' of the order » (M. SIMON, *Les sectes juives au
temps de Jésus*, Paris, 1960, 50, 51-52). See A. DUPONT-SOMMER,
« Le problème des influences étrangères sur la secte juive de Qumrân, » in RHPR 1, 1955, 75-92 ; ID., *The Essene Writings ...*, 39-67 ;

It is up to the experts to establish this point beyond doubt. Meanwhile, let us note that Philo stresses the importance that these ascetics attached to the inspired ethic whose content they discovered in Scripture. [36] This is how he underlines the earnestness of their common life :

> First, no house belongs to any one man ; indeed, there is no house which does not belong to them all, for as well as living in communities, their homes are open to members of the sect arriving from elsewhere.
>
> Secondly, there is but one purse for them all and a common expenditure. Their clothes and food are also held in common, for they have adopted the practice of eating together. In vain would one search elsewhere for a more effective sharing of the same roof, the same way of life and the same table. This is the reason : nothing which they receive as salary for their day's work is kept to themselves, but is deposited before them all, in their midst, to be put to the common employment of those who wish to make use of it. [37]

The Essenes were an active body. Elsewhere Philo, possibly embroidering on the facts, compares them with another, much more contemplative sect : the Therapeutae who lived on the shores of Lake Mareotis near Alexandria. [38] These pure contemplatives mainly sought tran-

---

P. BENOIT, *loc. cit.*, 118-121 ; G. VERMES, *The Dead Sea Scrolls...* 13-15 ; M. PETIT, *op. cit.*, 114-131.

36. Thus *Quod omnis probus ...*, 80-84 (M. PETIT, 201-205).

37. *Ibid.*, 85-86 (M. PETIT, 206-209 with note 1 of p. 206). Compare with the summary of the prescriptions of the Rule in A. DUPONT-SOMMER, *The Essene Writings ...*, 45.

38. On the doubts that have long been entertained regarding the historicity of these Therapeutae, see the excellent Introduction by F. DAUMAS, *De vita contemplativa. Introduction et notes*, series : *Les Œuvres de Philon d'Alexandrie* 29, Paris, 1963, 26-66. EUSEBIUS OF CAESAREA, *History of the Christian Church* II : 17, 1-23 (K. LAKE translation, Loeb Series, 1926) takes up Philo's description.

quillity and silence. [39] Unlike the Essenes, this community admitted women, who also took a vow of chastity, [40] and youngsters. Its main task was not work but contemplation and prayer. Hence each dwelling had its *monasterion*, a sacred chamber into which the member would withdraw in solitude « to accomplish the mysteries of the religious life. » [41] As a community, the Therapeutae were markedly different from the Essenes, and the difference should on no account be minimized. [42] But taken together, several features of their life show that, from the standpoint of religious aim, their basic intuition linked up with that of the Essenes. Although the Therapeutae strongly emphasized the importance of « seeking God » through wisdom and the intellect — but here Philo is perhaps projecting his own ideas [43] — one finds in this Alexandrian community on the shores of Lake Mareotis the same total relinquishment of material possessions, the same life of poverty,

---

39. See F. DAUMAS, *ibid.*, 47-48.

40. This is clearly stated in paragraph 68 which specifies that these virgins « have not observed chastity through constraint » (F. DAUMAS, 127). For the male practice of chastity, see F. DAUMAS, *ibid.*, 49-50, and especially M. BLACK, « The Tradition of Hasidean-Essene Asceticism : its Origins and Influence, » in *Aspects du Judéo-christianisme, colloque de Strasbourg 23-25 avril 1964*, Paris, 1965, 19-33 (31).

41. *De vita contemplativa*, 25 (F. DAUMAS 95, with the important note 1 on p. 94 ; see *Introduction, ibid.*, 36 : Philo uses the word *monastèrion* which does not appear again till the third century).

42. This is stressed by F. DAUMAS, *ibid.*, 55-58. See (for a broader account) G. VERMES, « Essenes - Therapeutai - Qumran, » in *Durham Univ. Journal 52*, 1960, 97-115 and J. ZORRILLA, « La comunidad Qumran - Terapeutas, » in *Cuadernos Monasticos 8*, 1969, 1-55.

43. M. J. LAGRANGE, *Le judaïsme avant Jésus-Christ*, Paris, 1931, in his Appendix on the Therapeutae, fears that Philo is doing just this !

obedience and chastity, [44] the same liturgical rites, the same common meals, the same love of prayer and zeal for the Law as distinguished the ascetics on the shores of the Dead Sea. [45] Hence we are once again faced with man's courageous effort to enter more deeply into the experience of the Covenant.

It is also known that among the Pharisees were men who lived in « brotherhoods » called *habhuroth*, and that

---

44. On this question of chastity, see G. W. BUCHANAN, « The Role of Purity in the Structure of the Essene Sect, » in *Revue de Qumrân* 6, 1968, 353-390 ; A. MARX, « Les racines du célibat essénien, » in *Ibid.*, 1970, 323-342 ; A. GUILLAUMONT, « A propos du célibat des Esséniens, » in *Hommage à André Dupont-Sommer,* Paris, 1971, 395-404 ; H. HUBNER, « Zölibat in Qumrân ? », in *NTS* 17, 1971-1972, 153-166. Pliny stresses the fact that the Essenes live « without women and renouncing love entirely, » and that into their community « no one is born » (*Hist. nat.* V : 17, 4, cf. A. DUPONT-SOMMER, *The Essene Writings...,* 37). Josephus writes that the Essenes « regard continence as a virtue..., disdain marriage for themselves, but adopt the children of others at a tender age in order to instruct them » (*Bell.,* II : 8, 2 ; A. DUPONT-SOMMER, 27). The extract from Philo's *Apologia pro Judaeis,* quoted by Eusebius of Caesarea, states that the Essenes « banned marriage at the same time on they ordered the practice of perfect continence ; indeed, no Essaean takes a woman » (*Praep. evang.,* VIII, 11 ; A. DUPONT-SOMMER, 25 ; the rest of the text reveals Philo's misogyny). Nevertheless, female remains have been discovered at Qumran. Was there a category of Essenes who permitted marriage ? (cf. F. DAUMAS, *op. cit.,* 55, which would be consistent with the statement of Josephus, *Bell.,* II : 8, 13 : « there is yet another order of Essenes : they agree with the others regarding the type of life and customs observed, but depart from them on the question of marriage. For they believe that unmarried people cut out a very important aspect of life : the propagation of the species »). Could there have been a female branch, as in the case of the Therapeutae ? Or a kind of Third Order ?
45. See the parallel index drawn up by M. SIMON, *op. cit.,* 107-113.

these had real affinities with the life style I have just described. [46] Whatever may be said of the latter grouping —
for some scholars have maintained that the Qumran community derives from the Pharisaic *habhûrah* [47] — we are
faced with an historical fact of the utmost theological
significance : namely, that within the People of God, [48]
some believers had decided to live together in order to
help one another to « seek God. » This is an undeniable
and acknowledged fact. An historical fact upon which
theology must reflect.

How can we best describe this religious endeavour, since
religion is undoubtedly involved here ? As a search for
communion with God, pursued not on the basis of ritual
practices but through a very precise life style. When one
reads and meditates the Qumran texts, the Damascus
Rule, the commentaries of Josephus and the writings of
Philo (who was perhaps deeply influenced by his own
ideal), one becomes convinced that, for the Jews in question, the aim was to make life so transparent to the Law
that it would be governed by the will of God. We have
already noted how profoundly the certitude of man's pov-

---

46. On ,the Pharisaic communities, see G. VERMES, *The Dead
Sea Scrolls* ..., 34-35, 65 ; L. FINKELSTEIN, *The Pharisees : the
Sociological Background of their Faith*, Philadelphia, 1966 ; J. JERE-
MIAS, *Jerusalem in the Time of Jesus*, London, SCM Press, 1969,
246-267 ; J. NEUSNER, *From Politics to Piety, the Emergence of
Pharisaic Judaism*, New York, 1973.

47. Thus Chaim RABIN, *Qumran Studies*, series : *Studia Judaica*
II, Oxford, 1957. See A. DUPONT-SOMMER, *The Essene Writings...*,
404-408.

48. On the link between the Jewish « sects » and the People as a
whole, see M. SIMON's perceptive remarks, *op. cit.*, 3-16.

erty cleanses this endeavour of all traces of pride. The undeniable legalism of some of these groups is steeped in a faith that vivifies it : the existence of each member becomes a homage to God and a proclamation of the greatness of his grace. The dimension of prohibitions, magic and fear of the divine is perhaps not wholly eliminated, but it does not exercise a major influence. The members do not thirst for extraordinary phenomena or « marvels. » The liturgical enthusiasm of the prayer of the Therapeutae and the Therapeutrides, as described by Philo, [49] is in no sense a frenzied over-excitement. Everything is geared to a « normal » human activity which is a response to God and thereby glorifies him. For both the activity of the mind engrossed in contemplation and that of all the human powers straining to obey God's commandments have as their ultimate end God himself. Moreover, if the Therapeutae do not appear to have been much preoccupied with messianism and eschatology, [50] the Qumran texts show that the preparing of « God's path » in the wilderness to hasten the coming of the eschatological times counted just as much as the destiny of the members of the sect. [51] In all things God comes first ! In other words, attentiveness to God and to his purpose matters more than anything else. That God is the Lord of Israel's faith. Even in the case of the Therapeutae, so attached to the joys of the

---

49. *De vita contemplativa* 83-89 (F. DAUMAS, 143-147). Here Philo speaks of dances, of divinely inspired rhythm, of the wine of friendship which he compares to that of the Bacchanalian feasts, of the women's enthusiasm at the crossing of the Red Sea, and of drunkenness.

50. See F. DAUMAS, *op. cit.*, 56.

51. *The Community Rule*, VIII : 14, G. VERMES, 85-86.

mind, the most striking feature is that they are « faithful followers of the Law, » [52] more religiously rooted in the precepts of Deuteronomy than in the speculative schemes of Greek philosophy, however much the latter may enthral them.

For these ascetics, attentiveness to God is embodied in a common life organized *around* it, *because of* it and *for* it. This point is essential, for the same internal law subsequently re-emerges in Christianity. We have noted that there are profound differences between these groups and that they do not easily fall under the same category. Yet in all of them the practical organization of the week or the day [53] is wholly subordinated to the aim of « seeking the God of Israel. » The meticulous regulating of their existence is meant to be both a proclamation of the vigour of this quest for God and a means of realizing the latter. For from the daily horarium to the distribution of duties, from the way of dressing to that of eating, from the obedient attitude demanded of all the members to the graded and established hierarchy, from the difficult entrance test to the gradual and communal initiation of the « postulants, » from the severity of the disciplinary code to the members' desire to be responsible for one another, from individual poverty to the sharing of goods and private incomes, from voluntary celibacy to the choice of a place favourable to the ascetic life, from

---

52. F. DAUMAS, *op. cit.,* 46-47. For the Essenes, see the summary drawn up by A. DUPONT-SOMMER, *The Essene Writings ...,* 51-54. See, from another standpoint, A. STEINER, « Warum lebten die Essener asketisch ? » in *Bibl. Zeitsch.,* 15, 1971, 1-28.

53. On the importance of the week in the time-table of both the Essenes and the Therapeutae, see M. SIMON, *op. cit.,* 109-110.

the silent meditation of the Scriptures to the community's divine worship, everything in this life style — despite variations depending on the particular outlook of each sect — is primarily determined in relation to the « quest for God. » These are groups consciously adopting an internal law of existence so conceived that their one and only preoccupation can be this « quest. » The common life is built around this preoccupation. If, especially in the case of the Qumran ascetics, there is a strong tendency to maintain that God can be truly served only within the sect, the aim underlying this « monastic » organization of existence is not to deny that God can be sought elsewhere. It is at once more humble and more great : to realize a life style, a way of fulfilling « the job allotted to man » that is centred on attentiveness to the God of the Covenant.

In speaking of the ideal of the Therapeutae, I mentioned the importance they attached to contemplation. I should, however, briefly point out the marked difference between this contemplation, described by Philo steeped in Hellenistic Judaism, and what I called earlier the contemplative moment in the call to « follow Christ. » The latter moment belongs to the domain of intuition ; it is wholly charismatic and given in the Spirit. I have described it as a doxological reaction, a need to worship : it echoes the discovery of the treasure or the fine pearl. It is a moment woven into the event of encountering Christ. An authentic « following of Christ » must of necessity be rooted in it. The tranquil contemplation of Philo's heroes, on the other hand, belongs to man's efforts to penetrate more deeply into the mystery of God. As a valuable strand of the « monastic » traditions — the most

valuable in the eyes of Alexandrian Judaism and, subsequently, of a long Christian tradition — it forms part
of that skein of religious acts, of « disciplines, » which
enable the human mind to deepen its communion with
the divine. [54] And it retains its traditional value as a disciplined search for God even when, as Philo does already,
one emphasizes its essential dependence on the grace that
makes it a foretaste of eternal joy, the purely gratuitous
gift of God. [55] Whereas the contemplative moment in
which the « following of Christ » is grounded leans more
towards pure faith, this tranquil, intellectual contemplation practised by the Ancients leans more towards religion. This explains why, depending on temperaments,
some forms of « religious life, » even Christian, will lay
emphasis on it, while others will feel less inclined to stress
it.

This remark on the meaning and direction of the contemplative activity, [56] and on the fact that contemplation
may belong to the sphere of religion and not necessarily

---

54. On this problem see R. JOLY, *Le thème philosophique des
Genres de vie dans l'antiquité classique*, Brussels, 1956 ; A. J. FES-
TUGIERE, *Contemplation et vie contemplative selon Platon*, Paris,
(1936 ; A. DIES, *Autour de Platon*, T. 2, Paris, 1937, 523-603
(especially 581-603) ; ID., *Le cycle mystique*, Paris, 1909 ; from the
theological standpoint, see G. TURBESSI, « Quaerere ... nell'ambiente ellenistico e giudaico contemporaneo al N.T. », 383-395 (who
frequently refers to B. GARTNER, *The Aeropagus Speech and
Natural Revelation*, series : *Acta Seminarii Neotestamentici Upsal-
iensis*, Uppsala, 1955, where the problem is nonetheless posed in
a broader perspective than that of contemplation).

55. This is well emphasized by G. TURBESSI, *ibid.*, 393-395.

56. The expression « contemplative activity » comes from Paul
VI's Allocution to the Council, 7 December 1965 (cf. DC, 63, 1966,
col. 61).

of faith properly so called, helps to clarify our reflection. The « monastic » institution (in the broad sense I have given it) has its roots in an ancient soil which, for centuries and centuries, mankind has ceaselessly tended, both apart from and within the People of God. Moreover, countless scholars have stressed the extent to which the vision of Pythagoras is discernible in Philo's remarks on the Essenes [57] and the Therapeutae, [58] as well as in the account left by Josephus. [59] And before leaving its mark even on the description of the primitive Christian *koinonia* given in the « summaries » of the Acts of the Apostles, [60] it very probably influenced the life style of the ascetics of Alexandrian Judaism. [61]

What we know of the life and doctrine of Pythagoras — through the prism of his disciples' doctrines [62] — allows us to measure this influence. [63] Pythagoras of Samos, who

57. Thus M. PETIT, *op. cit.*, 60-62, 108-110, 249-250.
58. Thus F. DAUMAS, *op. cit.*, 124-125 (note 3), 134-135 (note 4).
59. It « clothes the Essenes in the Greek style and more precisely in the Pythagorean style », M. SIMON, *op. cit.*, 68.
60. This influence on the « summaries » has been studied by J. DUPONT, *Etudes sur les Actes des Apôtres*, series : *Lectio Divina* 45, Paris, 1967, 505-509, 513-514, 517-518.
61. See M. SIMON, *op. cit.*, 106-107 ; also I. LEVY, *La légende de Pythagore de Grèce en Palestine*, Paris, 1927.
62. See R. JOLY, *op. cit.*, 33.
63. On Pythagoras see A. DIES, *Le cycle mystique*, Paris, 1909, 54-61 ; A. DELATTE, *La vie de Pythagore de Diogène Laerce : éd. critique avec introduction et commentaire*, in *Acad. Royale de Belgique, cl. des Lettres et des Sc. Morales et Politiques, Mémoires*, 2e série, T. XVII, fasc. 2, Brussels, 1922 ; A. J. FESTUGIERE, « Sur le De vita Pythagorica de Jamblique, » in *Rev. des Et. Grecques*, 1937, 470-494 ; R. JOLY, *op. cit.*, 21-52, 172-173 ; G. S. KIRK and J. E. RAVEN, *The Presocratic Philosophers*, Cambridge, 1957, 217-231,

fast became a legendary figure, resolved, towards 580 B.C.,
to « follow God » (*epomai Theô*), in other words, to make
the soul's passage to God his one preoccupation. He gathered to him disciples whom he initiated into contemplation in a distinctively ascetic community life. For his
adelphoi (brothers) had an ideal of « brotherhood »
(*koinonia, suggenai*) based on the certainty of belonging
to the same God, urging them to mutual devotion, and
embodied in the sharing of all possessions. These features
would be further emphasized by the Neopythagoreans. [64]
Celibacy, of which there is little evidence at the beginning
of the movement, was gradually to become an element of
what Plato, alluding to this Pythagorean tradition, calls
tropos tou biou, a « rule of life. » [65] I should add that, here
too, entry into the fellowship was effected in stages. The
candidate was tested for an initial three-year period during
which he had to prove his soundness and especially his
selflessness. Then, having given his possessions to the community, he was trained under the direction of a master for
a further five years. Only then could he take the habit.

Of course, « most of the Pythagorean elements are
found in the description of the Essenic community » left
by Philo. [66] And here Philo is a trustworthy witness, at
least in his general view of the sect. [67] Some experts have
made a similar comparison between the Pythagorean,

236-262, 307-318 ; P. JORDAN, « Pythagoras and Monachism, »
in *Traditio* 17, 1961, 432-441.
   64. See P. JORDAN, *art. cit.*, 438.
   65. *Rep.* 600 B. For the question of celibacy, see P. JORDAN,
loc. cit.
   66. M. PETIT, *op. cit.*, 61.
   67. *Ibid.*, 62.

Stoic, Neoplatonic and Ciceronian outlooks and the vision of « Christian » monachism which was to prevail several centuries later. [68] Besides, as I pointed out in the foreword, numerous Christian monks and religious are today discovering their own traits in the Eastern monachisms. [69] The impact of such comparisons on the theology of the *Sequela Christi* is obviously of extreme importance.

What may we conclude from all this ? We must at all cost avoid concordisms and simplistic conclusions. Before categorically affirming that this or that life style is indebted to another, we have to examine in depth each of the elements involved ; we have to measure the differences and note how one surpasses the other or breaks away from a continuous tradition. The similarities cannot be explained solely in terms of direct dependence. The reappearance of identical circumstances can bring about a resurgence of the same communal attitudes. And indirect dependence, by way of literary traditions, is a constant phenomenon.

Reflecting on the question not as historians but as theologians, we must be content to note astonishing similarities without being too certain of the causes. But it is

---

68. Thus P. JORDAN, *art. cit.* (especially 439-441).

69. See the works cited above, note 18. For a rapid but thought-provoking presentation of these forms of non-Christian religious life, see P.D. CHANTERIE DE LA SAUSSAYE, *Manuel d'histoire des religions*, Paris, 1904, 391-396 ; G. F. MOORE, *History of Religions*, vol. 1, New York, 1916, 89-92, 286-300 ; J. GONDA, *Les religions de l'Inde*, II - *L'Hindouisme récent*, Paris, 1965, 38-39, 87-88, 97, 224-225 ; A. BARBEAU, *Les religions de l'Inde*, III - *Bouddhisme, jaïnisme, religions archaïques*, Paris, 1966, 21-24, 129-137, 198-200, 267-269.

perhaps not wholly by chance that the Christian monasteries in the wilderness of Judah sprang up more or less where the Qumran settlement stood, [70] that the Christian monasteries of Egypt flourished in the desert of Nitriae where the Therapeutae described by Philo sought God, that the Syrian Rules of Rabbula (c. 412 A.D.) show a resemblance to the Dead Sea texts, or that Eusebius of Caesarea recognized in the Therapeutae the ancestors of the monachism of his day. [71] In the view of one of the best experts on Judaeo-Christianity, it is conceivable that the Essenes really were the precursors of the Christian ascetic and monastic tradition, and that the Alexandrian ascetics provided a link between those Palestinian origins and the extension of Christian monachism to the Western Mediterranean countries. [72] Others believe that Christian monachism drew abundantly on Greek mystical philosophy and cite, as evidence of this osmosis, the fact that the *Encheiridion* of Epictetus was attributed to St Nilus and, under his patronage, helped to form generations of

---

70. See Derwas S. CHITTY, *The Desert a City*, Oxford, 1966, especially 13-16.

71. *History of the Christian Church* II : 17, 1-23 (SC 31, 72-77). For the Rules of Rabbula see M. KRETSCHMAR's contribution to the Strasburg Colloquium (23-25 April 1964) *Aspects du Judéo-christianisme*, 33.

72. M. BLACK, *ibid.*, 31-32. Discussing this question with M. KRETSCHMAR, M. BLACK « notes ,that the Essenes could have been, at least partially, absorbed by the Church. They could have introduced into the Church their own common life ... Christianity is an original phenomenon. But after 70 A. D. the Church could have undergone the influence of these Jewish sectarian groups by absorbing them, and could have given a Christological foundation to pre-existing ascetic practices » (*ibid.*, 33).

monks. [73] In this matter as in others, the existing documents do not allow us to reach definite conclusions.

Be that as it may, one thing is certain and well-established. The « monastic » life, considered in both its most classical forms and its derivatives, « is a human, therefore universal, fact which presents the same common traits in every clime. » [74] It is a religious fact. A path cut in countless cultures with a view to « seeking God. » A value of mankind which, as is all too obvious, the « following of Christ » welcomes. It is not faith — the faith of the Old Covenant or that of the Church — which accounts for the monastic life. Nevertheless faith embraces that life by bathing it in its own light.

In this perspective, how can we explain such a thirst for communion with the divine, manifested *in* and *by* man's very existence, on the grounds of a precise life style and not on the basis of ritual practices ? By recognizing that, hidden in the inmost depths of the mystery of man, there is an area of responsiveness to God which is neither fortuitous nor added to man's being but inherent in it.

Of course, this is a much-debated question. Some experts on the subject hesitate to reach conclusions, while others are affirmative. As is well known, Freud, in his book *The Future of an Illusion*, considers the notion of God to be superfluous, a pure illusion by which men make their unhappiness bearable, an interiorized image of the human father created by the needs of the unconscious. The emi-

---

73. On this *Encheiridion* of Epictetus (in the Works of Nilus, PG 79, 1285-1312), see J. QUASTEN, *Patrology*, T. 3, Westminster, 1960, 504.

74. A. J. FESTUGIERE, « Sur le De Vita Pythagorica de Jamblique », 478.

nent psychiatrist Viktor Frankl, reacting to Freud's view
in his study *The Unconscious God,* shows that, on the
contrary, the « desire for God » has objective roots. Far
from envisaging religion as a «collective neurosis,» Frankl
believes that the dismissal of religion leads to and finds
expression in « individual neuroses. » [75] And « if God
haunts the dreams of his patients, sometimes obsessively,
he sees this less as the persistence of an illusion than as
Jacob's struggle with the angel. » [76] For in Frankl's view,
one has to recognize the existence of a « spiritual unconscious » which is governed not by the pleasure principle
but by the « will to meaning » (what does my life *mean* ?)
and which « points to God. » [77] Beneath the immanent *I*
lies hidden a transcendent *Thou* whom the unconscious
strives to reach. [78] It is this longing for God which is
moulded into the elements proper to each religion and
each confession. Frankl speaks as a technician challenging
Freud's theory. But a theologian, considering the question
from the orthodox Freudian standpoint and speaking explicitly as a Christian has written these very profound
lines while commenting on Ricœur's study of Freud :

> If God's desire for man lies at the source of human existence,
> man's movement towards himself (i. e. his urge to explore
> and recognize himself) must necessarily bear the mark of that

---

75. Thus V. FRANKL, *The Unconscious God,* New York, Simon
and Schuster, 1975, 70.

76. Marcel NEUSCH makes this point in his Introduction to the
French translation of V. FRANKL, *The Unconscious God* (see above).

77. See chapter 6 of *The Unconscious God,* 60-70 ; also by the
same author : *Psychotherapy and Existentialism,* New York, Washington Square Press, 1967.

78. *The Unconscious God,* 37, 61.

desire and he must be able to decipher it, at least in principle. God's desire for man and man's desire for God cannot be fundamentally alien to that desire of God for man in which human existence is grounded. The movement of man striving to reach his own self cannot be radically alien to the movement in which human existence has its origin. Strictly speaking, it is contradictory to affirm that God's desire for man is at the source of being and to claim at the same time that this desire cannot possibly be inscribed, deciphered or bound up with the human desire for God which man's movement towards himself implies. The will to be myself, to name myself, cannot be wholly foreign to the way in which God desires and names me. Man's desire for God cannot be radically denounced as futility if it is in the Father's name that he is named. [79]

Despite the fundamental difference between their systems of reference, these two views link up with one another in their intuition. While admitting that the problem is complex, one cannot lightly disregard that intuition. The religious desire is the mark of origin on origin. [80] Just as the human navel, writes Frankl, « points beyond the individual to his origin in his mother, conscience can only be fully understood as a phenomenon pointing to its transcendent origin. » [81]

In this light the « monastic » aim becomes clearer. It has nothing to do with a morbid desire to deny oneself or a neurotic consent to alienation. On the contrary. That aim lies at the heart of the dynamic urge which carries man towards himself in his desire to live his true manhood, and which implies his acknowledgment of his relation to God. It is a truthful aim in which man finds himself

---

79. J. POHIER, *Au nom du Père ... Recherches théologiques et psychanalytiques*, series *Cogitatio fidei* 66, Paris, 1972, 60-61.

80. J. POHIER, *ibid.*, 59.

81. V. FRANKL, *The Unconscious God*, 54.

by seeking God. For since man is created and contingent, « he can recentre himself only by decentring himself in order to discover himself in what is his true centre. » [82] This is neither a refusal to live one's human destiny nor a timorous retreat from reality, but the will to give full scope to one's acknowledgment of God, without whom man cannot recognize himself « in truth » nor « truly » be born to himself. [83]

The « Following of Christ, » the Search for God, the Monastic Aim

Let us return to the « following of Christ. » Clearly, the religious quest for God takes on a different colour when it is assumed into man's enthusiastic self-surrender to the One whom he recognizes as the whole meaning and purpose of life. Here the sphere of « religion » — with what I called the « monastic aim » as its central preoccupation — becomes constructional material for building up the wonder of faith. For the act of faith,

82. See J. POHIER, *op. cit.,* 59, together with the very perceptive and prudent analyses of A. VERGOTE, *Psychologie religieuse,* Brussels, 1966, especially 155-212.

83. « Origin cannot be foreign to its own source, and the contingent human being cannot recognize himself without recognizing that upon which he depends. So not only is the recognition of self achieved by means of the recognition of the other, but it discovers itself in the recognition of the other and, so to speak, springs from it » (J. POHIER, *ibid.,* 57).

considered mainly under its contemplative aspect, forms
the pivot of existence.

Fundamentally, it is a matter of having to answer the
call of Christ, which suddenly resounds in the life of a
Christian « seized with joy » at the sight of the fine pearl
or the treasure. The « search » is no longer the first con-
sideration, as it is in the monachisms of the non-revealed
religions. In Jesus, God has manifested Himself. So it is a
question of responding to a gift, of endeavouring to enter
into his welcome. What I said earlier about Paul is applicable here. I leave everything because I prefer the Lord
to everything else. But in order to embody in time-dura-
tion the charismatic event of this encounter with Christ,
the *kairos* of this God-centred decision, I incarnate its aim
in a « religious » style of existence. In the wholly God-
centred « Yes » of profession, I decide to distance myself
from the normal object of my instinct to possess, of my
amorous desires and of my will to power. Thanks to my
wholly « religious » Rule of life, I give myself the means
of concretizing this decision. In a manner of speaking, I
institutionalize the event of my decision born of faith. I
thus enable my daily life to be a realistic « Amen » to the
Lord Jesus. As in all « monachisms » and kindred forms of
life, it will be a question of seeking communion with God,
but on the basis of an *already* which is the capturing of
the person by the Lord Jesus. And this puts a wholly new
complexion on the matter.

In these circumstances, the religious quest for communion with God, pursued in reference to the One whom
the seeker is following, becomes a modelling of the self
on Christ. Did not Jesus, through his whole existence,
ceaselessly and courageously « seek communion with the

Father » ? The whole of John's Gospel affirms that he did. Contrary to what our habitual ways of conceiving christology imply — for they are implicitly monophysite in their one-sided emphasis on Jesus' divinity — the One in whom the Christian faith recognized the eternal Son of God after the Resurrection showed himself to be, in fact, the messenger, the Servant of God, eager to do God's will by communicating with every fibre of his being in the divine purpose. And God is the Father. Now, having considered them earlier on, we all know the verses of Philippians where Paul describes the path of his life (a path opened up by the Damascus event) as an entry into the mystery of Jesus thanks to a fellowship that extends to *koinonia* in His sufferings and death. The « following of Christ » leads to the « imitation of Christ » in the strong sense in which Paul understands this expression. [84] It is true that in the New Testament the « following of Christ » describes the act of leaving everything because one has been seized by Christ, whereas the « imitation of Christ » is more expressive of having a relationship with the Father that echoes Jesus' relationship with Him. [85] The imitation is more moral, more « religious. » But we now see how « following » and « imitation » hinge with one another in the religious project, even if « imitation » is of a higher order.

By this very fact, the specifically religious aim of the

---

84. See C. SPICK, « L'imitation du Christ, » in *Théologie morale du Nouveau Testament*, T. 2, Paris, 1965, 688-744 ; R. THYSMAN, « L'éthique de l'Imitation du Christ dans le Nouveau Testament ; situation, notations et variations du thème, » in ETL 1966, 138-175.

85. *Devant Dieu et pour le monde, le projet des religieux*, series : *Cogitatio fidei* 75, 167-168.

« search for God » assumes new overtones which essentially characterize Christianity. It is the religious aim which basically distinguishes Christian monachism (and its derivatives) from the other forms of monastic life, including those of the Essenes and the Therapeutae. For in Christian monachism the search for God can only be carried out *en Christô*. Through his Holy Spirit, Christ is at once the cause, the field and the model of the *true* « religious » attitude, including its most profoundly human characteristics. This forces on us the question of the economy of the Incarnation.

For what we discover here is well and truly the human effort to find God, as genuine as the search pursued in the Pythagorean communities or in the monasteries of India but, this time, intrinsically bound up with what God has revealed about himself in Jesus Christ and man has accomplished for himself. The *en Christô* is penetrating. The human remains inviolate, its dignity remains intact. Yet its density is penetrated by the fire of the Spirit which illuminates it and gives it a new meaning. In the brotherly *koinonia* the mark of a God revealed as Trinity shines through like a fine filigree. In poverty and asceticism one perceives the surging vitality of the kenosis of Christ, « who was rich but became poor » (2 Co 8, 9) and « emptied himself » (Ph 2, 7). In obedience one hears the echo of « I have come down from heaven, not to do my own will, but the will of him who sent me » (Jn 6, 38). In chastity there is a glimpse of the mysterious words : « unless a grain of wheat falls into the earth and dies, it remains alone ; but if it dies, it bears much fruit. He who loves his life loses it, and he who hates his life in this world will keep it for eternal life » (Jn 12, 24-25). In these circumstances, what was human effort — man's plodding effort translating the nobility of his destiny — becomes a « memorial » of the grace (*charis*) of God unfolded in Jesus Christ, the *sacramentum* of « gratuitous » Salvation. Asceticism itself — understood in the broad sense — ceases to be simply moral : it is bound up with the Cross so that the wholly God-centred quality of the Cross runs through it. Ultimately, the boundary line between religion and faith becomes so porous that it is almost invisible. Where, in the life of Francis of Assisi, does penance cease and the joyful confession of the Cross begin ?

Is this « following of Christ » charismatic ? Yes. What accounts for it, long before human merit, is the radiant joy of being captured by Christ and his Spirit. But I cannot stress too often that all this has nothing to do with charismatic « phenomena » and their « marvels and wonders » aura. Here we are on a different plane : that of existence guided by the Spirit, of man's everyday life with its very realistic demands, his life led *en Christô*.

Is this a second-grade charisma ? No. In this matter the intuition of popular piety has been unerring. The *Legenda Aurea,* the *Fioretti,* the lives of the saints, the naive hagiographies (such as we read them in the 2nd Nocturns of the Roman Breviary) have perceived the link between the sanctity of their religious heroes and the power of the Spirit within them. That piety has multiplied miracles, popularized « marvels and wonders, » and embellished reality with a profusion of extraordinary « phenomena. » An irritating device, one must admit, but rich in its theological intuition. The popular hagiographers were translating into a « charismatic » language their conviction that these heroes were men of the Spirit.

On this point it is enlightening to compare the expression « second baptism, » which in the old texts designates religious profession, with the expression « baptism in the Spirit » as used by pentecostal and kindred groups. Elsewhere I have outlined the history of the phrase « profession — a second baptism » and shown how it has become hardened by usage. [86] In the course of time, the rites of profession have managed to copy, as it were, the ritual of baptism by developing some of its elements. But even in its most exaggerated expressions — as evidenced by Bernard, who goes so far as to speak of « re-baptism » [87] — the concept always implies a second conversion. On the basis of the gift of baptism, the one baptism which is not meant to be renewed, the religious endeavours to live the full implications of this unrepeatable gift. In fact, he is not « re-baptized, » but « re-immersed in baptismal conversion. » What he seeks here is the evangelical quality of existence, the role of the man who responds to God's call, and not the renewal of the gift of the Spirit. His gift has been received once and for all in the sacraments of Christian initiation ; and it is deepened by communion in the Body of the Risen Lord, who is « filled with the Holy Spirit. »

Now, the pentecostal « baptism in the Spirit » places the accent elsewhere. [88] Certainly one must make a clear

---

86. *Ibid.*, 304-313.

87. See the text quoted *ibid.*, 310.

88. On this baptism in the Spirit, see the excellent book by James D. G. DUNN, *Baptism in the Holy Spirit*, in *New Testament Library* series, SCM Press, 1970, who examines the problem from the exegetical standpoint ; also ID., « Spirit-Baptism and Pentecostalism, » in *Scottish Journal of Theology* 23, 1970, 397-407.

distinction between the meaning it has assumed in the Pentecostal groups in the strict sense, who are associated with the denominational Pentecostalism that flourished at the beginning of this century, [89] and the meaning that certain Catholic groups propose to give it today. [90] But a theologian long involved in the « Catholic charismatic renewal » has had the opportunity to note (without perhaps sufficiently qualifying his remarks) that the origins of the rite may well leave their mark on the celebrations of those Catholic groups. For, he points out,

> here we have a veritable pentecostal ritual. However ancient may be the rite of imposition of hands in prayer, and whatever may be its possible interpretation, it comes to us in this instance from a pentecostal practice that risks carrying with it its own

---

89. On this denominational Pentecostalism and its conception of « Baptism in the Spirit, » see especially Nils BOLCH-HOELL, *The Pentecostal Movement ; its Origin, Development and Distinctive Character*, Oslo, 1964 ; D. GEE, *Wind and Flame*, Croydon, 1967 (revised edition of *The Pentecostal Movement*, Croydon, 1941) ; J. HOLLENWEGER, *Enthusiastisches Christentum, die Pfingstbewegung in Geschichte und Gegenwart*, Zurich, 1969 (English translation with important historical and bibliographical additions : *The Pentecostals*, London, SCM Press, 1972).

90. For this interpretation given by Catholic groups, here are a few titles selected from a vast literature on the subject : E. O' CONNOR, *The Pentecostal Movement in the Catholic Church*, Notre Dame, Ind., 1971 (with bibliography ; Father O'Connor was to distance himself from the movement, disturbed by its theological orientations) ; Kevin and Dorothy RANAGHAN, *Catholic Pentecostals*, New York, 1969 ; Donald GELPI, *Pentecostalism, a Theological Viewpoint*, New York, 1971. As an example of a very critical reaction of a former promoter of the movement, William Storey, a Professor of Liturgy and Church History, see « Interview with Professor William Storey, » in J. R. BOUCHET and H. CAF-FAREL, *Le Renouveau charismatique interpellé, études et documents*, Paris, 1976, 93-134.

private significance, independently of the practitioners' Catholic-sounding explanations. Today we are becoming increasingly aware that rites cannot be handled anyhow, and that their content always transcends whatever we may say about them. Can one, in this case, borrow such a significant rite from the tradition of denominational Pentecostalism without equally carrying off with it at least some of the theology which it conveys ? (...) Now, what we do know about the link between the laying-on of hands and the theology of baptism in the Pentecostal ritual is precisely this : according to the Pentecostals, at the moment of the imposition of hands the Spirit is, so to speak, « liberated » in man. [91]

Hence there is a tendency to believe inwardly — whatever may be asserted publicly — that this « baptism » must be understood « less as a renewal of (the) profession of faith than as a rite whose purpose is (...) to obtain the fullness of the Spirit and perceptible manifestations of his power. » [92] Moreover, even in certain Catholic groups, it is sometimes expected that, in the case of a « normal » candidate, the effects of the outpouring of the Spirit will make themselves felt immediately after, or even during, the laying-on of hands. [93] It is hoped that « charisms » will be received, and notably the gift of tongues : something has just got to happen. Consequently, in such cases,

after having received « baptism in the Spirit, » the person who does not begin to « speak in tongues, » and does not experience inwardly that profound transformation described in all the writings of the « Charismatic Renewal, » is frequent-

91. J. R. BOUCHET, *ibid.*, 26-27 (especially 22-31).
92. H. CAFFAREL, *ibid.*, 63-64 (pp. 62-66 are of special interest and should be read as a whole).
93. This is underlined by J.R. BOUCHET and H. CAFFAREL, *ibid.*, 27-28, 64-65.

ly surprised and disturbed (this applies as much to priests and religious as to the lay participants) ... The experience, they feel, has probably been thwarted by some inner obstacle, some wrongful tendency perhaps, a sin, a « bondage ». [94]

If this is really the case, the contrast between this « second baptism » in the Spirit and the « second baptism of profession » is all too obvious. The pentecostal « baptism in the Spirit, » even when the recipients are mainly concerned with its inward effects, is too heavily dependent on « charismatic phenomena » with their aura of « marvels and wonders. » Religious profession, for its part, aims at another level of experience : that of the « charismatic life » and its normal substance. Here I agree with, and venture to quote, a distinguish expert on « spiritual movements » :

> At no time has the Catholic tradition claimed that a rite automatically and unfailingly produces tangible supernatural effects : this applies as much to the reception of the sacraments as to the great acts of the Christian existence (religious profession, for example). [95]

---

94. H. CAFFAREL, *ibid.*, 65-66.
95. H. CAFFAREL, *ibid.*, 65.

III

Studied in the context of the New Testament and in reference to the Church's Tradition, the « following of Christ » has therefore revealed its charismatic aspect. It is truly a « life in the Spirit. » And here as much emphasis must be laid on *life* as on *Spirit.* Following Christ involves living in a way that is thoroughly penetrated by the experience of the fine pearl and the treasure — a charismatic experience, if ever there was one. In the circumstances, the monastic aim, which springs from one of the noblest desires which the Spirit has ever awakened in man's heart — the desire to « seek God » — is pursued with a view to embodying in the day to day routine the follower's enthusiasm for Jesus, who is inseparable from his Father and his Gospel. The will to inject the confession of Jesus Christ into the very root of human desire — at the point where it branches out into the desire for possessions, sexual desire, and the desire for self-affirmation — thus dominates and colours a particular form of human existence. And all this is dedicated to the service of the Gospel.

The Confession of Faith as a State of Being : Witnessing among Men, before God

The group of apostles who followed Jesus on the roads of Judaea and Galilee, making him and his word the deepest preoccupation of their lives, appropriated the confession of faith as a permanent *state of being*. In their encounters with their fellow-men, what I have described as adoration did indeed become confession of faith. Not the confession of « apostolic preaching » or of « kerygmatic proclamations, » but of the orientation of one's whole life *because of* Jesus. Paradoxical as it may seem, I would say that this was the first apostolate, preceding and conditioning the sending forth of the apostles by the Risen Lord. In the new times opened up by the Resurrection, the religious who follow Christ — so totally convinced that he is the one thing necessary that they dedicate themselves to him together with the forces and basic drives on which their individual humanity depends — also make the confession of faith a *state of being*. Their decision, a doxological and adoring response, leads on to a life experience which is a confession of Christ. In other words, it is by their way of life that they are witnesses. This is their first apostolate. Like Peter and the sons of Zebedee, they obviously do not follow Christ *in order to* bear witness. Nevertheless they follow him, witnessing *at the same time*. For their whole existence is one of witness because of the profound motivation that governs it. Witness flows from the very nature of their existence, and inevitably, rather like smiling is inherent in man's nature, as the Scholastics would say. Witness is the glory of their existence. Life witness is the splendour of the *state* of confession of faith. Before God that state is adoration ; among men it is witness, even before it is made explicit in a *verbal* confession of faith.

Such witness embraces and inseparably unites what the person has *become because of* Christ and what he *does because of* this new life. For what I said earlier about the doxological value of action is equally applicable here. Once again I must emphasize the falseness of the axiom (fast becoming a cliché) that what matters is being, not action. The actions whereby Peter and the sons of Zebedee commit themselves *because of* Jesus are intrinsically bound up with their person and witness to the attraction he exercises on them. But I would like to make this point quite clear. I am not speaking of what the apostles verbally « relate » about their Master, or of the objective content of their message. I am speaking of what Paul Ricœur describes, in a penetrating study, [1] as « action itself in so far as it testifies externally to the inner man himself, to his conviction and his faith, » [2] « the orientation of a life » in so far as it provides, by itself, « the

---

1. Paul RICŒUR, « L'herméneutique du témoignage, » in E. CASTELLI, *Le Témoignage, Actes du colloque organisé par le Centre International d'Etudes Humanistes et par l'Institut d'Etudes Philosophiques de Rome*, Paris, 1972, 35-61. This study is summed-up and sentences from it are almost literally reproduced in P. JACQUEMONT, J.P. JOSSUA, B. QUELQUEJEU, *Le temps de la patience, étude sur le témoignage*, Paris, 1976. The authors acknowledge their indebtedness.
2. P. RICŒUR, *op. cit.*, 43.

sign, the living proof of a man's conviction and devotion
to a cause » [3] : in short, the witness's involvement in his
action. Even, if necessary, to the point of dying for his
belief. Martyrdom becomes the test of this total entry of
the witness (*martus*) into his conviction. In other words,
the actions whereby the person commits his entire life
to the cause that animates it are the testimony he bears to
that cause.

Many pages of the New Testament convey this conception of the witness. In fact, in John's Gospel (when compared with the Synoptic Gospels or the Acts of the Apostles with their emphasis on the activity of proclaiming the
Good News), « the balance clearly swings from the narra-
tion pole to the confession pole, » [4] and the vocabulary of
witness (*martureô*) prevails over that of proclamation. [5]
Jesus witnesses to the Father through his life, which is
sealed by the martyrdom of the Cross. The Apostles witness to Christ Jesus by the way in which the cause of their
Master and Lord consumes their lives, even to the point
of martyrdom. Following in their footsteps, the religious
witnesses to Christ by the way in which he integrates
into his « profession » and the acts that flow from it the
conviction that the Lord Jesus is the be-all and end-all of
man's existence. That conviction underlies the traditional
parallel between religious profession and martyrdom. [6]
Both are unsurpassable instances of a committed faith in
Christ : in both cases the believer risks his life. As for the

----

3. *Ibid.*, 43.
4. *Ibid.*, 48.
5. See especially P. JACQUEMONT, etc., *op. cit.*, 73.
6. See J.M.R. TILLARD, *Devant Dieu et pour le monde*, 290, 307.

religious, his entire existence — including its roots and its « works » (*erga*) and the words which will disclose the meaning of the message — is seized by the conviction in which it is grounded. So much so that it merges with this conviction.

To place existence — being and action — before the spoken word. To place the *state* of confession before the *word* of confession. To raise a question by the mere fact of the osmotic relationship between the conviction that quickens one's life and the shape the latter is taking through its commitment to this conviction ; and only then to answer the question. This is surely the primary role of all religious in the service of God's Kingdom. That service will subsequently take the path of proclamation, the *spoken* confession. But will the latter be credible if it is not the verbalization of a conviction already incarnated in a life ?

This witness of lived experience, which is called to blossom into an explicit « proclamation » to mankind, cannot be genuine unless it is borne *before* God. This point, which I have always stressed because I believe it to be essential, [7] is endorsed in a thought-provoking study recently published by three Dominican brothers : *Le temps de la patience.* [8] Admittedly, the preoccupation of these co-authors differs from mine : they are concerned with the dilemma of communicating faith, the difficulties of bearing witness, the firm refusal to « win over » others to their cause, the absence in our world of a « pointer to

---

7. See the title of the book just quoted, footnote 6, and page 299-304 in the same work). Also my article « Mission et missions : l'Evangile, » in *Vocations* 1973, 83-100.

8. See note 163 above.

faith. » But taking their bearings on the thought of Paul Ricœur and of Kierkegaard, they explain why the audience, the « public » — therefore those to whom the apostle is « sent » — is not competent to assess the witness of Christians in the proceedings between God and the Prince of the World, before the tribunal of history. [9] The public is not the judge in these proceedings. Its reaction cannot possibly be « the criterion for judging the authenticity of this testimony and therefore the goal directly pursued by the witness. » [10] For, writes Kierkegaard, « while the witness's *communication* is addressed to his contemporaries, the witness addresses himself to God and makes Him the authority. » [11] Our three authors comment on this thought of Kierkegaard as follows :

> God is the authority because I address myself to him alone, I commend myself to him alone ; my responsibility as a witness is discharged before God, not before you others. Not before you to whom I am addressing my message (...) Like faith, like prayer, witness is borne *before God* even if, like faith itself, it is realized through action in the world (...) You are not the authority, nor are you the judge. But because preaching undoubtedly involves crisis and judgment, it is you who are judged — by God who is the authority. Still, if I address myself to God, it is not only so that I may feel responsible before him alone, but also because I place myself in his hands. Similarly, if we say that he judges, it is also because we believe that he is grace, for without him no one can accept the message : only through him does one accept it. He is grace and, in this, he is the supreme authority. As St Augustine says, it is

9. See P. RICŒUR, *op. cit.*, 50-52, and P. JACQUEMONT, etc., 72-73.

10. P. JACQUEMONT, etc., *op. cit.*, 130.

11. S. KIERKEGAARD, *Journals and Papers*, Indiana U.P., 1967, vol. I, 314.

the inner word of the Master which reveals to ,the listener's heart the meaning of the witness's word. [12]

Now, I would hesitate to affirm categorically that the witness's responsibility « does not aim to obtain » the listener's response. [13] But I do agree that the witness is not responsible *before* that listener, and that fundamentally his responsibility cannot be measured by the latter's response. The witness is responsible *before* God, who mysteriously associates the « gratuitousness » of witness with the « gratuitousness » of his own grace.

This is true of every witness to the Gospel, but it is especially true of the one who « follows Christ. » *Because of* Christ, he witnesses *among* men, but *before* God. Thus, even on the plane of witness, we can more clearly perceive the essential link between what I called the contemplative moment of the *sequela Christi* — the God-centered splendour of being seized by Christ — and the moral, «religious» style — the path of the « search for God » — which the believer adopts in order to incarnate his fidelity to that moment. Kierkegaard tells us in some very closely knit passages [14] that the gospel « message » should be « reduplicated » in the existence of the witness, and that his existence is the only valid exposition of that message. For « Christianity is an existential message, » and not merely a doctrine. The « following of Christ » represents one form of this « reduplication. » To quote the authors of

---

12. P. JACQUEMONT, etc., *op. cit.*, 133.
13. *Ibid.*, 133. The meaning of this clumsy expression is subsequently clarified, *ibid.*, 140.
14. Those cited by P. JACQUEMONT, etc., *ibid.*, 131-132 ; see also J.M.R. TILLARD, *Devant Dieu et pour le monde*, 333-334.

Le temps de la patience, with apologies for taking this passage out of its immediate context, the following of Christ strives to achieve

> a certain quality of life, a deepening of existence which immediately lends weight to the word — one « hears » from what depths the words spring — and subsequently represents the only possible sign of this word's power, its efficacy. [15]

For it aims to reach the secret meeting-point where the gift of God and the longing for God join up in the very existence of the believer and of the whole People of God.

The classical assertion that the religious life has a prophetic function merely confirms and sums up what I have just attempted to explain. Since I have underlined the traditional parallel between religious profession and martyrdom, it is useful to recall that although prophetism of the « charismatic phenomenon » type was evidenced in the primitive Church, [16] the wave of prophetic « manifestations » gradually ebbed. [17] It was the confessors and the martyrs who then became the vehicles of the Spirit of witness in their « sufferings unto death » inseparably linked with the inspired words they uttered in the power of the same Spirit. [18] In them too we perceive the *state* of

---

15. P. JACQUEMONT, etc., *op. cit.,* 158.

16. See James D.G. DUNN, *Jesus and the Spirit,* 227-233.

17. See M. LODS, *Précis d'histoire de la théologie chrétienne du IIe au début du IVe siècle,* Neuchâtel, Paris, 1966, 64-71. See, from another standpoint, J.L. ASH, « Decline of Prophecy in Early Church, » in *Theol. Stud.* 37, 1976, 227-252.

18. See M. LODS, *op. cit.,* 80-86. Also ID., *Confesseurs et martyrs successeurs des prophètes dans l'Eglise des premiers siècles,* Neuchâtel, Paris, 1958 ; M. PELLEGRINO, « Le sens ecclésial du martyre, » in *RSR* (Strasbourg) 35, 1961, 152-173.

witness, the Spirit at work in existence itself, preceding and authenticating the utterance of the man of the Spirit. Of course, we must avoid anachronisms and not exaggerate the comparison between religious profession and martyrdom, but we must keep this evidence in mind when we speak of the prophetic function of the religious life. Some scholars even maintain that the cenobitism that flourished from the fourth century onwards grew out of the martyrdom of the first centuries. [19]

The Confession of Faith in the Service of Humanity, before God

The « following of Christ » leads into a *state* of confession of faith, a plane of existence against which the *words* of confession stand out in bold relief. Now, an essential component of this Christian existence is the service of mankind, in the name of the Gospel, because of Jesus Christ. Among the religious families which constitute the orders and the congregations this service is variously stressed.

Here I am not discussing the case of strictly eremitic personal vocations, which the Church's legislation hesitates to consider as « religious » unless they are, in one way or another, linked with a « common life. » I am merely noting that every form of the *sequela Christi* leads

19. A point also made by O. CLEMENT, *Questions sur l'homme,* Paris, 1972, 95.

to the service of mankind. Even the most monastic and the most contemplative. [20] And it is not simply through their prayer, their constant intercession and their time-honoured hospitality that the contemplative orders serve their fellowmen. Nor merely through their traditional charity to the poor, as evidenced even among the monks of old who lived in the wilderness. [21] Nor solely because their habitual labours are those of simple, ordinary men — peasants in their fields, craftsmen in their workshops — or of scholars straining their eyesight as they decipher the documents of history. No, it is also because the climate of solitude and peace, the silence, the discipline and the austerity which they try to establish in their monasteries or cloisters represent true values for the world. Precious values which are in peril. Areas of human life without which our societies would rapidly suffocate.

In the case of the more modern Congregations or Institutes, however, the « subsidiary aim » which embodies their apostolic purpose is usually one form or another of more directly « social » service. The service they give — whether it be the care of the sick and of the poor, teaching or education in the broader sense — is undoubtedly social. Clearly, this responsiveness to the needs of mankind has steadily increased over the last few centuries, and to such a degree that, as I said earlier, the good works of the religious community have, in many cases, become its all-embracing if not its chief preoccupation. In fact —

---

20. See *Devant Dieu et pour le monde, le projet des religieux,* 428-445.

21. See the examples quoted in my article « La pauvreté religieuse, » in NRT 102, 1970, 931-934.

and despite the danger I have pointed out, this is one of
its titles to fame — the religious life has gradually taken
upon itself what the first centuries called the *diakonia*.
And it is not by chance that in the Reformed Churches
and the Anglican Communion, the terms diaconate and
deaconess have been spontaneously chosen to designate
the revived forms of the religious life. [22]

To follow Jesus in the new times opened up by his
Resurrection is, in fact, to follow him on the path of his
Lordship, even if that path inevitably involves communion
in his suffering and his Cross. The « search for God, »
which the religious project both undertakes and embodies,
implies a decision to conform to the Father's will by
entering into another conformity : communion in the attitude of Jesus. Now, throughout his ministry, from his
baptism to the Cross, Jesus never ceased to link up the
proclamation of the Kingdom and the message of Salvation with the fulfilment of the signs of the Kingdom. The
signs by which human distress and oppression are overcome. [23] For, unlike the Baptist, Jesus conceived his ministry in terms of Salvation rather than of judgment. [24] He
wished to be the Servant of the Father and of his plan for
mankind, a plan entailing the care of the poor and the
advent of a world of justice and peace : for God owes this
to the glory of his name. [25] Having become the Lord of

---

22. See M. HILL, *The Religious Order*, London, 1973, especially
143-150, 179-180. See also *La Diaconesse*, Series : *Etudes du Conseil
œcuménique* No. 4, Geneva, 1967.
    23. See James D.G. DUNN, *op. cit.*, 53-62.
    24. *Ibid.*, 60-61.
    25. J. DUPONT shows this clearly in *Les Béatitudes*, T. 2, series :
Etudes Bibliques No. 87, Paris, 1969, 65-90 (especially 79-90); see

history, Jesus now works on mankind through his Spirit, until the day when « he hands over the Kingdom to God the Father, having done away with every sovereignty, domination and power » (1 Co 15, 24) and will be subject in his turn to the One who subjected all things to him « so that God may be all in all » (15, 28). The chief event of the end of history will coincide with this handing over of the Kingdom to the Father. It will be the definitive moment of the establishment of God's Reign [26] : God (inseparable from his plan) is the ultimate end, Christ is the penultimate. [27] For Paul, history advances towards that day when Christ « will present himself before the Father to announce the fulfilment of his mission. » [28]

It is with this mission, carried out in the Spirit of the Resurrection, that Christ associates the men and women whom, since his Passover, he has constantly called to « follow him. » *Because* of him, they leave everything and go, not on the roads of Galilee, but in the workyards where mankind is preparing its future. *Because* of him, they enter into the service of God's plan. There is no need to stress the fact that, as in life witness itself, it is *before* Christ and his Father that they are responsible. Not *before* the world. Although they commit themselves *for* the world, it is always *before* God that they do so. But how ?

---

also J. JEREMIAS, *New Testament Theology*, Vol. 1, *New Testament Library* series, London, 1972, 108-121 (especially 112-113).

26. See C.K. BARRETT, *The First Epistle to the Corinthians*, London, 1971, 356-357.

27. *Ibid.*, 357.

28. TOB, 518, note y.

When God's project is read with the breadth that the Bible gives it from the Genesis narratives to the visions of the Apocalypse, it does not merely concern the other-world salvation to which mankind must be awakened by receiving the word of faith that leads to eternal life. It equally bears on humanity's destiny in this world : man's dignity calls for another kind of world. Hence the success of man's world, the world which the generations build and to which they devote their greatest efforts, matters to God. This world of ours, the one discussed in the newspapers, today, must *already* become the world that God desires, in anticipation of that mysterious moment when Christ « will hand over the Kingdom to God the Father. » The themes of justice, human development, brotherhood, truth, the freedom to live wholly as a man therefore belong to God's plan. Today we are more clearly aware of this. In consequence, the path of Christ's Sovereignty is marked out by the projects of men, their challenging of situations of injustice and oppression, their efforts to build a society consonant with the dignity of man, God's « royal creature. »

Religious follow Christ in this concrete universe, where at this moment of history the success or failure of the divine plan, the growth or stagnation of the Kingdom of which he is Lord are in the balance. Today they are, of course, doing this in a new way. In former days their charity attended to the needs for which the secular society made no provisions, and in the jungle of life they opened up wide clearings for the humanist or technical culture of the time ; today it is becoming more and more a charity of solidarity with the currents of salvation that are flowing through humanity and channelling its hopes. What was once private charity is becoming social in the wider sense. But the basic, evangelical intuition that inspired so many founders and foundresses when they dedicated their Institute to the service of charity nonetheless remains intact. New « subsidiary aims » have been and are being constantly adopted to meet the needs of our evolving societies. The path that stretches from « the liberation of prisoners captured by the Muslims » to « solidarity with the oppressed workers » is a long one, yet it is always the same path.

Now, in the « following of Christ » this work *for* the world, undertaken *because of* the Lord Jesus and *before* God, assumes that note of gratuitousness which, as we noted earlier, characterizes witness. Here the religious does not attempt to win anyone over to his cause. Even if no one saw or understood the meaning of his action, he would still feel obliged (because of his responsibility *before* God) to change the world by his efforts. Even if all mankind, having understood the message and turned to God, were awaiting eternal life, he would still fulfil his duty of making the world more consonant with the will of God. This is something he owes to God. And it is in the adoring, doxological response to Christ Jesus that what is known as the « subsidiary aim » of the religious order is boldly written. For it is a responsibility *before* God. Of course, all Christians share this responsibility, but in the case of religious the decision to « follow Christ » makes it a particularly serious responsibility. For since religious inject the confession of Christ into the very roots of the three great drives of the human personality — sexuality, possessiveness and the power complex — their action itself necessarily bears the mark of the absoluteness of this decision.

The action of religious, whatever may be its sphere in a complex world, is rooted in that absolute decision. Consequently, its primary objective is not to satisfy the general law of « work or starve » through a realistic identification with the situation of most men. Certainly the religious accepts this law but he sets it in a broader perspective. Similarly, his basic motivation is not compassion at the sight of the alienation of the exploited masses or on beholding all the distress that has to be relieved. That compassion — which is real and genuinely evangelical — is bound up with a deeper preoccupation. And last but not least, his action is not meant to be purely edifying, seeking merely to provide a platform for the « message » thanks to a calculated and somewhat crafty *captatio benevolentiae*. For just as existence *before* God is of value in itself, even before the spoken word that clarifies its meaning to the observers, action *before* God has its own weight and depth, even before the word interprets its significance.

We should note that, particularly in the case of the religious families known as the « active » orders, a « spirituality based on action » cannot seek its inspiration elsewhere than before God. Every activity pursued by a religious in the joy of his decision to follow Christ is, in fact, permeated by this relation to God and his Kingdom. Even as it is directly aiming to achieve purely secular or profane objectives which give hardly any glimpse of the supernatural, it is straining towards God. It can be imbued with an ardent love of God. Contemporary exegesis, which on this point links up with a patristic current of thought represented, among others, by John Chrysostom and Ephraem, [29] refuses to read in the pericope of Martha and Mary (Lk 10, 38-42) the suggestion that, in terms of charity, Martha's practical service is inferior to her sister's attitude. [30] The Lord's words of praise refer not to Mary's general attitude but to one of its aspects ; her attentiveness to « the word which calls us to faith and commitment. » [31] Commenting on Luke's pericope, the Dominican Louis Chardon wrote in 1647 :

> The very object of the contemplation of Mary is the subject of the activity of Martha. Jesus, however, is not divided. He is all Mary's and all Martha's ; and as he belongs to both, they also both belong to Him. The testimonies by which they protest their love for Him are united in the same indivisible centre in which two distinct lives are referred to one and the same Person. [32]

And further on he adds that Martha's action has a truly contemplative aim, for « if she leaves her contemplation to pay attention to her action, still she does not leave the subject of her contemplation. Though she changes her exercise, she does not change the subject of that exer-

---

29. On this point see the very enlightening study by D.A. CSANYI, « Optima pars. Die Auslegungsgeschichte von Luk 10, 38-42 bei den Kirchenvätern der ersten vier Jahrhunderte, » in *Studia monastica* 2, 1960, 5-78. See also I. HAUSHERR, « Utrum S. Ephraem Mariam Marthae plus aequo anteposuerit, » in *Orientalia christiana* 86, 1933, 147-167.

30. Thus E. LALAND, « Die Martha-Maria Perikope Lukas 10, 38-43. Ihre Kerygmatische Aktualität für das Leben der Urkirche, » in *Studia Theologica* 13, 1959, 70-85.

31. TOB, 231-232, note t.

32. Louis CHARDON, *The Cross of Jesus* (1647), London, Herder, Vol. II, 184.

cise. » [33] The activity of religious *before* God has this quality of Martha's attitude *before* the Lord. It is not a distraction from praise and contemplation, even if the mind is explicitly applied to practical matters.

The reference to God and to his plan, however, makes certain specific demands on the activity by which religious seek to transform the world in fellowship with their Christian brethren. Obviously, God's will regarding man and his world bears less on the saga of progress as such, a kind of Promethean conquest of the universe, than on the quality of man and his life. Consequently in the very midst of the human enterprise from which it benefits, the whole People of God has a word to say and to incarnate about man, even if it is not always possible to name its source to others, who will come to that knowledge only gradually. And this word rebounds, like an echo, at several levels.

Let us call to mind at random just a few of those levels which more directly concern religious. First there is the level of values : the duty of placing in their right order the priorities which are usually those of our societies but hardly correspond to the vision of man-as-God-desires-him, the vision revealed in Jesus :

> Today, as in the time of those who conversed with Jesus, our scale of priorities gives first place to the goods that we consume or wish to possess, then second place to good human relationships — if we have time to foster them — and the last place to good relations with God, but only if there happen to be a few gaps in our time-table... [34]

33. *Ibid.*, 184.
34. G. MARC, *Passion pour l'essentiel* (*essais*), Paris, 1967, 127.

and... if we happen to believe in him. Now Jesus rejected this age-old scale of values, centred on the desire to get rich and to get on. He gave first place to man's relationship with the other person :

> the « wholly other » who is God, but also this other man, my friend or my enemy, whom I can name, and by extension this people, this social class, this age group, this trade union, this political party which are not mine. What is sub-human in man is translated today, as in primeval times, by fear of the other, the one who differs from me and in whom I do not recognize myself. [35]

By virtue of their project, religious strive to reconstitute Jesus' scale of values which our modern societies have turned upside down. This enables them to perceive another essential trait of the man-whom-God-desires : the rejection of a situation where fear of the other is exorcized by setting up « a hierarchized system of oppressive relationships, » a reign of brutal force and of the falsehood that Solzhenitsyn stigmatizes. But religious know that, in the Gospel, love is clearly

> more than the overcoming of oppression, more than neutrality, and far more than defenceless resignation. It is a prodigious movement of the will to die unto oneself and to foster the growth of the other person, even one's enemy... It is by placing oneself under the dependence of the other that one grows, not the other way round. This incredible way of acting is the exact opposite of what men have done spontaneously whenever the question of sharing wealth arose in our society. It is this dying unto oneself which is the way of salvation, of restoration, of regeneration. Certainly it implies a reversal, a conversion of the relationships between human groups. [36]

---

35. *Ibid.*, 178.
36. *Ibid.*, 154.

If, through the mediation of the Christian community, our humanity, stupefied by its mortal, frenzied greed, can learn what kind of man it is that God desires, clearly the small handful of religious, together with all Christians, must play a role in this awakening.

The reference of religious to the man-whom-God-desires involves an even deeper level of existence. The aim of the divine plan is that this world, which men must build in love, should open a way to the « God who is all in all » of the Day of the Lord (1 Co 15, 28). This leads the Christian community to believe in its own heart, then to show others, that even the greatest achievements cannot satisfy mankind's profound yearning as long as it has not recognized its God. Such a demonstration is a positive criticism, gratefully acknowledging the slightest sign of goodness or truth but refusing to see it as the attainment of the goal, for the world is meant to proceed much further. It is as if humanity were steering for a port and the criticism of God's People made that port constantly recede, obliging it to go further. Through its positive criticism, the Christian community makes the goal visible in the light of a quality of soul — of persons and societies — which transcends the improvement of our material standard of living, transcends our historical liberations, and even transcends death. If ever the day dawns when all injustice will have vanished from the face of the earth, the Christian community will still continue to call men to enter ever more deeply into the realm of Hope :

> What I have in mind is the City's openness to the presence of God, to the miracle of his Incarnation, whose aim is not just a « happy » man but a « blessed » man, ripened in the sun of the Beatitudes, even if he is persecuted, a martyr... All

things are subordinated to the Kingdom, not merely to the natural exploitation of the earth, and certainly not to the calm acceptance of their place in history, but to their transfiguration into the « new earth. » This entails no transference, no flight to the beyond, but a change of goal : the transcending of penultimate values in an attempt to reach the final, ultimate values. [37]

From the State of Confession of Faith to the Word of Confession

Still, the « following of Christ » on the path of his Lordship cannot be satisfied with action alone : it has to *say* something about God and Jesus Christ. We have seen that the witness's existential *state* of confession has to be made explicit through a *word* of confession. So too must his action, which is an essential aspect of his witnessing existence and which he undertakes *before* God so that man may become what God desires him to be. The disciples who followed Jesus on the paths of his ministry, and Paul dramatically flung on to the roads of the Mediterranean world, proclaimed the Word. Although the *state* of confession — embracing being *and* action — has its own weight and depth prior to any *word* of confession, it nevertheless needs that word so that the faith which it embodies may be aware of itself and live. The arcane discipline which Dietrich Bonhoeffer recommended to his contemporaries, and which is often necessary today, always seems

---

37. P. EVDOKIMOV, *L'amour fou de Dieu*, Paris, 1973, 141.

harsh to the believer. Yet in the very pursuit of that discipline the believer is expressing his faith : he is confessing it to his brothers, and to God in liturgical prayer. [38]

Indeed, faith needs to proceed to the word. A spoken word, obviously : a word man listens to and welcomes. The whole of the New Testament shows beyond doubt that its central statement, « the confession of Jesus as Lord, » must not only be lived but communicated, passed on, attested, « with the irrepressible force of Good News, a joyful rumour. » [39] Faith has to be expressed, circulated. Faith is made to hear the echo of its own affirmation : if it is deprived of speech, it dies. It ceases to be lived experience from the moment that the believer becomes incapable of saying something about Christ whom he loves and serves. This does not imply militancy or the believer's determination to impose his faith on others. He remains on the objective plane, for faith has an intrinsic need for objectivity : « the word of faith is not preserved by being hoarded ; it cannot increase unless it is spoken and communicated. » [40] That is why the religious, who builds his existence around the contemplative moment which I described earlier, cannot avoid *expressing* (in words) the faith that lives in him. So, fundamentally, this confession of faith has a doxological value : it resembles the lover's desire to speak of his loved one, whose love has turned his world upside down. A gratuitous, unselfish desire.

---

38. Here I am taking up a few ideas already expressed in *Religieux sur les chantiers des hommes,* Brussels, 1975, where I have developed this theme. Basically, they tie up with the thoughts of P. JACQUEMONT, etc., *Le temps de la patience,* although the context is different.

39. J. MOINGT, « La transmission de la foi, » in *Etudes* 342, 1975, 107-129 (108).

40. P. JACQUEMONT, etc., *op. cit.,* 139.

Nevertheless, [41] the *before* God, the state of being in
which the religious lives his « following of Christ, » does
inject into this doxological confession of faith the keen
desire that others, hearing his word and the message it
contains, should also come to follow Christ. There are two
main reasons for this. The first is that no Sovereignty can
be fully realized unless it is acknowledged : hence the
desire to see the greatest possible number of men welcoming the word of faith. And the second is that the true
service of man, the man-whom-God-desires, makes this
adherence essential. For to lead man to the explicit worship of God is to love him supremely, since it means freeing him from his ignorance concerning his ultimate destiny
and sometimes liberating him from an alienating idolatry
(centred on an ideology, for example, or on a material
situation) in order to open him to the one valid absolute.
The Christian community therefore has the responsibility
of making the *because of* Christ, which motivates it and
commits it to the hardest building tasks of mankind, flower
into an *in the name* of Christ. And if this « *in the name
of* » is to be more than just a slogan, Christians must,
sooner or later, manage to spell out its content : the re-
minder of the day when Jesus died on Golgotha to rise
again in the glory of his Lordship and divine sonship.
Only Christians can speak this language : here we have
« one of the purposes of the Church for which no agency
of society will make itself responsible if she fails in her

---

41. Here I hesitate to associate myself with the view of the
authors of *Le temps de la patience*, as I feel that their statement
must be much more carefully qualified : they appear to have over-
looked the two points which I am underlining and which are essential to the balance of the gospel life.

task. » [42] And if she did fail, all would lose by it : men would be no longer reminded of their true end and shape their lives accordingly ; believers would no longer reveal their faith to one another and to themselves by expressing it in words ; and — let us state this boldly — God himself and his plan for mankind would no longer be fully served.

Clearly, religious and nuns perform, within the Christian community, a special role in this witness to Christ which emerges from the Christian existence considered in all its depth and breadth, from the quality of an individual life to the general commitment to serve mankind. Their existence, which serves humanity *because* it has been seized by Christ, undoubtedly represents in the Church a privileged locus for the « uttering » of faith as a lived experience. Moreover, it is not by chance that throughout history monks and religious have often been pioneers in the missionary endeavour, in the task of evangelization entrusted by Christ to his People, and in the work of catechesis and religious education.

Indeed, the religious project makes the faith-inspired motivation which quickens the People of God and underlies its testimony stand out in bold relief. It is significant that in the gospel narratives (as in the subsequent tradition) the group that follows Jesus emerges as a signature, a token, a symbol of the first community of believers, the community gathered before Pentecost. Probably because this group evidences with a kind of steel-like clarity the conviction and the irresistible urge which fill those who

---

42. B. BESRET, *Tomorrow a New Church,* New York, Paramus, Toronto, Paulist Press, 1973, 31.

adhere to Christ. Through the position it takes, because of Jesus, regarding the basic spheres of life (family, occupation, possessions...) it pins down, then writes out in capital letters, the faith of the whole community of disciples. True, all the followers of Jesus carry this conviction in the inmost depths of their being : when they are compelled by circumstances, they all yield to the demands that such a conviction implies, including martyrdom. But because of its readiness to face risks and its enthusiastic attachment to the living core of their faith, the group that follows Jesus from village to village becomes, as it were, the symbol of that place held by Jesus in the existence of the whole community of disciples and believers. In this little group the signature « Jesus » stands out in capital letters. Capitals so bold and clear that they force themselves upon all observers. Now, analogically, the same holds true of religious and nuns in relation to the whole Christian community. The religious and his lay brothers and sisters have the same faith, the same will to bring into being the man-whom-God-desires, the same fidelity extending, if necessary, to martyrdom. In short, the same certainty of belonging to Christ. But in the case of the religious, who has injected the confession of Christ, as man's absolute, into the deepest roots of his existence, the main roots, this signature « Jesus » is written in capital letters. The fact that he voluntarily leads a life which differs somewhat from that of the average layman causes Christ to stand out clearly and sharply as the one Lord of existence, the only one on whom the believer stakes both his personal happiness and his commitment to the transformation of the world. Here we find an « all or nothing » outlook on life, the audacities of a certain impatience, a determination not to conceal the evidence. The religious firmly underlines the reference to Christ as Absolute. Admittedly, the writing of a statement in small or capital letters in no way changes its content ; a whole sentence may be written in one or the other and the content remains absolutely identical. But the sudden use of capitals enables us to perceive at a glance the key-word, the word that lends its tone to the proposition.

Bearing in mind the importance of « uttering the word » which confesses the faith incarnated in life, it is fairly easy to discern and understand the function of the vows, a point we have already covered in the previous chapter. But it is often less easy to disclose the function of action, especially when the work undertaken by the religious is not a specifically ecclesial task, such as pastoral care, preaching, catechesis, works of charity, and the like. Many religious pursuing one form or another of secular work are troubled by this problem. Yet the awareness of the « *before* God » of action, and the meaning that the « *before* God » confers on action, provide an answer to their problem.

For, today, religious are working in the very heart of the world and participating in social projects because Christ urges them to do so. It is for the Gospel that, individually and collectively, those who are obliged to abandon the works that belong to an earlier stage of history are now choosing new ways of fitting into the social realities of our time. They are taking up this work because of Christ. In order to « follow » him, in this world, on the paths of his Sovereignty. The situation would not be the same if, toiling in these new environments and applying themselves to unfamiliar tasks by force of circumstances or because of the need to earn a livelihood, they were at the same time ardently striving to witness to their faith. For they are going where action is needed because of a deliberate wish to go there, an explicit and calculated choice, rarely imposed on them by force of circumstances or the need to earn a living, and always governed by their specific project, or at least closely linked with it. The radical nature of the commitment to Christ, which has torn them away from the usual way of living the human adventure, even the good Christian way of the layman, influences and underlies this decision. By that very fact, their active integration into the most secular tasks, provided that it is lived in an absolutely clear-minded fashion, assumes a particular colour : the one which, arising from the depths of their action for man carried out *before* God, enables the Church to state her kinship with the Lord and his Gospel more confidently and boldly.

Doubtless the Christian community should be the first recipient of this message. The word of faith of religious — from the most contemplative to the most active — cannot be spoken solely by them, but must find an echo in the word of faith of their fellow Christians. The complementarity of vocations in the Body of Christ makes this essential. For in the same way that no gift of the Spirit is ever made to one man alone, no vocation is ever realized by a single individual. Hence the confession of Jesus Christ and of his Father, the expression of a lived faith, life witness, the question posed to man which obliges him to face another, decisive question — in short, the *state* of confession that religious reach because of the wonder that Christ awakens in them — seek to be made explicit within and by the Christian community, and in a *word* that is at once confession and « proclamation. »

These are indeed the ways of the Spirit. The fact — an essential one, in my view — that the *state* of confession of faith, which distinguishes the religious life, normally proceeds to the *word* only within and through the Christian community is a clear sign of this action of the Spirit. Here our experience is that of the Body of Christ, in which the Spirit who apportions his gifts makes all Christians responsible for them and intends them to benefit the whole community. Indeed, it is not a matter of seeking marvellous « phenomena » but of fostering the growth, in life itself, of a charism centred on faith and its most typical sign : the « Yes » to God and his plan, in Jesus Christ, uttered wholeheartedly, by the whole person. As we have seen, that person has been captured both in his being and in his royal vocation : the building up of a world worthy of man. The fact that it is the Christian community as such which has to interpret and express the significance of an existence led along these lines proves beyond doubt that the authentic Christian endeavour is miles away from the sectarian temptation which can easily beset spiritual movements too obsessed with « marvels and wonders, » a religiosity tinged with magical thinking and superstition, or the thirst for « signs of God » in everyday life. [43]

---

43. See J.R. BOUCHET and H. CAFFAREL, *op. cit.*, 139-142 (text by H. CAFFAREL).

By way of conclusion, let us recall that it is in the God-centred, contemplative, adoring, doxological moment that the « following of Christ » is formed and blossoms. The wonder-filled welcoming of the One who passes by, and *because of* whom the disciple leaves everything, the « religious » institution, coming down to us from the dawn of history and structured around the common search for God, the witness to lived experience borne *among* men but *before* God, the responsibility of cooperating in the building of a new world, the explicit proclamation of the *word* of faith — all these elements of the « following of Christ » penetrate one another. None of them can be taken in isolation. The « Yes » which this man or woman once said to Christ Jesus as he was passing by permeates their whole existence...

> On two separate occasions Peter received the call, « Follow me. » It was the first and last word Jesus spoke to His disciple (Mark 1, 17 ; John 21, 22). A whole life lies between these two calls. The first occasion was by the lake of Gennesareth, when Peter left his nets and his craft and followed Jesus at His word. The second occasion is when the Risen Lord finds him back again at his old trade. Once again it is by the lake of Gennesareth, and once again the call is : « Follow me. » Be-

tween the two calls lay a whole life of discipleship in the following of Christ.

Halfway between them comes Peter's confession, when he acknowledged Jesus as the Christ of God. Three times Peter heard himself proclaim that Christ is his Lord and God — at the beginning, at the end, and at Caesarea Philippi. Each time it is the same grace of Christ calling Peter to follow, and revealing itself to him in his confession.

This grace was certainly not self-bestowed. It was the grace of Christ Himself, now prevailing upon the disciple to leave all and follow Him, now working in him that confession which to the world must sound like the ultimate blasphemy, now inviting Peter to the supreme fellowship of martyrdom for the Lord he had denied, and thereby forgiving him all his sins. In the life of Peter grace and discipleship are inseparable. He had received the grace which costs. [1]

Now, this costly grace, this *Yes* which will lead him « where he does not wish to go, » is for Simon Peter and for every religious *the* charism which makes existence as such a sign of the Gospel. This charism comes from the Lord's Spirit. It is not a second-grade charism awaiting other manifestations which alone would entitle the disciple to belong fully to the world of the Spirit. It is truly a gift made by the Risen Lord, through his Holy Spirit, to his People. The Lord passes by... His grace seizes certain men and women. Poor sinners, they are nonetheless of those who will say to their brothers and to the world : « We have found what we were looking for ! Come and see !... » This is their charism. Tiny and frail when set in the vast context of the Church's life. In no sense exceptional or « miraculous. » But like an April bud on the old tree of the Church...

1. D. BONHOEFFER, *The Cost of Discipleship*, London, SCM Press 1948, 39-40.